HOW TO GET I.D. IN CANADA

HOW TO GET I.D. IN CANADA

AND OTHER COUNTRIES

RONALD GEORGE ERIKSEN 2

Loompanics Unlimited
Port Townsend, Washington

HOW TO GET I.D. IN CANADA

Printed in U.S.A.

Published by:
Loompanics Unlimited
PO Box 1197
Port Townsend, WA 98368

Typesetting and layout by Patrick Michael

ISBN 0-915179-13-X
Library of Congress Catalog Card Number: 84-81635

Contents

Contents

And that no man might buy or sell, save that he had the mark, or the name of the beast, or the number of his name.

The Revelation of St. John the Divine

Introduction

At various times in my life, I have worked as an auto-repossessor, a private process server, and as an unlicensed private investigator.

During the course of my work, I located several thousand people who, for one reason or another, did not want to be found.

Much misfortune befell these people once they were found. Some of them had their cars repossessed. Others were served legal papers and were endlessly hassled by unscrupulous attorneys and creditors. Still others were thrown in jail.

Almost all of these people could have avoided all this grief if they had just changed their names and taken a few simple precautions.

Although there have been several books written on how to get false identification papers in the United States, nothing has been written on how to get such documents in other countries. This book will show you how to get fake I.D. in Canada, Mexico, and many other countries. This information will enable you to hide from anybody who is looking for you.

Nowadays, everybody should have a good set of fake I.D. One never knows what the future holds. Any number of bad things could happen to you.

- War could be declared for real or imagined reasons and you might be drafted.
- Martial law could be declared. People without the "right" papers could face harsh penalties.
- You might be told you are an illegal alien and ordered to go back to where you came from.

These and any number of similar situations could dramatically change your life for the worse. By getting fake I.D. now, you can minimize many of the problems that the majority of sheep in our society will face.

How to Get a Canadian Birth Certificate

In Canada, even more than in the United States, the birth certificate is the key piece of I.D. Once a birth certificate in somebody else's name is obtained, you will be able to get any other I.D. you want in that name. The best way to obtain somebody else's birth certificate is through the infant identity method.

The infant identity method will allow you to establish solid, long-term fake I.D. *In this method, you take over the identity of a child who was born around the same time you were, but who died early in life.* Finding such a child and the information you will need to obtain the birth certificate (date and place of birth and the parents' names) is a fairly simple task. All of this information can be found through one or more of the following research techniques: 1) Looking through the obituaries of old newspapers. 2) Looking through the death records in a vital statistics office. 3) Looking at cemetary headstones. Let's take a detailed look at each of these research techniques.

Old newspapers: Here you would look through the obituary section of old newspapers for dead children who match your age, sex and race. Microfilm of old newspapers can be found in many public libraries or at the main office of the newspaper.

If you look through the newspaper editions put out during holidays, you will notice a lot of fatal traffic accidents. This is because there are more people on the roads and also because of the greater percentage of drunk drivers. Although it may seem gruesome or ghoulish, news accounts of these incidents are ideal for finding a deceased child who matches your age, sex and race. Also, they are particularly good for finding children who died far away from home.

Vital statistics offices: Looking through the death records in a provincial vital statistics office is the fastest way to find a suitable dead child. Unfortunately, the bureaucrats in charge of these records often do not allow the general public access to them. A ruse may be necessary to gain access to these records. Two time-tested ruses are to claim you are a genealogist or a student doing medical research.

Some large cities require the purchase of a burial license before the deceased can be buried. The burial licensing agency often has its own set of records similar to those in the vital statistics office. The people in these offices are often not as vigilant as the people in charge of vital statistics.

Cemeteries: Here you would tromp through cemeteries looking at the gravestones for a child who died early in life.

On many stones, you will see something like "John J. Doe, April 1, 1960 - June 6, 1966." Sometimes the parents' names will also be on the stone.

Obtaining the Birth Certificate

To obtain the dead child's birth certificate, you will need to know the child's full name, the date and place of birth, and the parents' names.

If, after doing your research, you don't have all this information, you will have to write for the death certificate first. The death certificate has all the information you will need on it. All that is needed to obtain death certificates is the child's name and date and place of death.

Birth and death certificates are issued by the provincial vital statistics office in each province's capital city. Some vital statistics offices have a form to be filled out when applying for birth and death certificates. In actual practice, however, if you send your request in a letter with the information mentioned above, they will send you the certificate without your having to fill out a form.

Listed below are the addresses for each province's vital statistics office.

Alberta
Vital Statistics
10405 100 Avenue
Edmonton, Alberta
T5J 0A6
Fee: C$3.00

British Columbia
Division of Vital Statistics
1515 Balanshard
Victoria, British Columbia
V8W 3C8
Fee: C$5.00

Manitoba
Vital Statistics
Room 104
Norquay Building
Kennedy & York Sts.
Winnipeg, Manitoba
R3C 0V8
Fee: C$5.00
Make checks payable to
Minister of Finance

New Brunswick
Registrar General of
Vital Statistics
Dept. of Health & Welfare
Room G72
Centennial Bldg.
Box 600
Fredricton, New Brunswick
E3B 5H1
Fee: C$3.00

Newfoundland
Vital Statistics Division
Dept. of Health
Confederation Bldg.
St. John's, Newfoundland
A1C 5T7
Fee: C$5.00

Northwest Territories
Vital Statistics
Government of Northwest
Territories
P.O. Box 1320
Yellowknife, Northwest
Territories
X0E 1H0
Fee: C$3.00

Nova Scotia
Vital Statistics
Dept. of Health
Provincial Bldg.
Halifax, Nova Scotia
B3J 2M9
Fee: C$5.00

Ontario
Mrs. R.E. Dratkin
Registrar General
McDonald Block
Parliament Bldg.
Toronto, Ontario
M7A 1Y5
Fee: C$5.00

Prince Edward Island
Director of Vital Statistics
Dept. of Health & Social Serv.
P.O. Box 3000
Charlottetown,
Prince Edward Island
C1A 7P1
Fee: C$5.00

Quebec
Registrar General
Population Registrar
Dept. of Social Services
845 Joffre Ave.
Quebec City, Quebec
G1S 3L8
Fee: C$2.00

Saskatchewan
Division of Vital Statistics
3475 Albert Street
Regina, Saskatchewan
S4S 6X6
Fee: C$5.00

Yukon
Registrar General of
Vital Statistics
Box 2703
Whitehorse, Yukon
Y1A T6C
Fee: C$3.00

The reason that the Infant Identity Method is the best way to go in obtaining false identification papers is that the birth certificate and all subsequently obtained I.D. are legitimate, official government documents.

If a government or private investigator were to investigate your identity, he would find no evidence that you are not who you claim to be. The only ways you could be exposed as a fraud are: (1) The investigator contacted the dead child's parents; (2) You opened your big mouth and told an unreliable person who you really are; (3) The birth and death certificates were cross-referenced.

Rumors, Rumors, Rumors

There is a rumor going around that Canada has cross-referenced all birth and death records. I have no idea as to how this rumor got started, but it just isn't true.

I contacted two provincial vital statistics offices, the Registrar of Canadian citizenship, and the Canadian passport office, and nobody at these places knew anything about cross-referencing of birth and death records.

I personally know of a person who has obtained everything from a birth certificate to a passport under a different name. If such a cross-referencing system were in effect, surely this person would have been caught.

Canada has always stamped "deceased" on the birth certificates of those infants who died at or near birth. Also, the government keeps a record of those people who have legally changed their names. This is the only type of cross-referencing that I have found.

In the future, Canadian "authorities" just might decide to cross-reference birth and death records on the provincial level. To protect yourself against this possibility, try to find a child who was born in one province and died in another.

The ultimate protection against cross-referencing is to find a Canadian child who died outside Canada in another country. *No records of death are kept on such people in Canada. The death certificate is issued only where the person died.*

To find such a child, go to your local public library and look at the annual encyclopedia yearbooks under "Disasters." Under this heading, you will see a rundown of various plane crashes, floods, avalanches, etc. Your best bet is to find a Canadian aircraft that crashed in the U.S. When you find such an event, you would then look at newpaper microfilm accounts of the crash. Usually the newspaper lists all the people who died in the crash. Once you find a suitable child, you would then research the information you need to obtain the birth certificate. Remember, in such a case, the death certificate would be in the U.S., not Canada.

Getting Supporting I.D. in Canada

Once you have secured a birth certificate, you will need to get some supporting I.D. Both the driver's license and the social insurance bureaucrats require one other piece of I.D. in addition to the birth certificate.

They really don't care what the other I.D. is as long as it has your name on it and looks good.

Here is a list of some easily obtained supporting I.D.:

Club membership cards: There are thousands of clubs throughout Canada. They range from animal welfare leagues to political organizations. Many of these clubs issue membership cards. One needs only to join the club to get the card.

Library cards: These are easily obtained, usually with no questions asked.

Student I.D. cards: Most colleges issue I.D. cards for their students. Simply register for a class and then go get the I.D. card.

International Student Identity card: This I.D. card is available from Council on International Educational Exchange, 205 E. 42nd Street, New York, NY 10017.

Medical I.D. cards: These list any severe allergies or unusual blood types that you might have. They are available from many pharmacies and hospitals. You can get one by simply calling or writing to the International Association for Medical Assistance to Travelers (IAMAT), 123 Edward St., Suite 725, Toronto, Canada M5G 1E2.

Blood Donor card: If you donate a pint of blood to the Red Cross in Canada, they will send you out a nice I.D. card.

Hunting and fishing licenses: These are available in most sporting goods stores. No I.D. is required to get them.

Automobile titles: Automobile titles are very impressive documents. Just go to any junk yard and buy the cheapest wreck you can find. Then get the title transferred to your new name.

Provincial I.D. cards: Some provinces issue I.D. cards for people who are unable to drive. These are even easier to obtain than driver's licenses.

Mail order I.D.: There are all sorts of bogus I.D. you can buy through the mail. You can get anything from college diplomas to birth and baptismal certificates. A good book on the subject is *I.D. For Sale*, listed in the "Recommended Reading" section.

Costa Rican passport: Got an extra $96,000.00 laying around? If so, a firm in Costa Rica can get you a Costa Rican passport. Briefly, their scheme is that you "invest" the money in their local hotel and they will get you the passport. You will also have to pass a security check. For more information, write: El Punto Costaricense S.A., P.O. Box 90, Paseo Estudiantes, San Jose, ZP 1002, Costa Rica.

World Service Authority: The World Service Authority issues a "passport" and "World I.D. card." Suprisingly, these documents can get you into such places as Zambia, Upper Volta, and Yemen with no additional I.D. For more information, write World Service Authority, 1300 Connecticut Avenue, #307, Washington, D.C. 20036, U.S.A.

Make your own: The book, *"How Driver's Licenses Are Made With the Polaroid Camera"* shows you how to make almost any kind of I.D. that you want (see Recommended Reading).

How to Get a Canadian Driver's License

More so than even the social insurance card, the driver's license is the most universally accepted piece of I.D. If you have ever tried to open a bank account or been questioned by police types, you know that the first thing people ask to see is your driver's license. People who don't have a driver's license are generally regarded as social pariahs and outcasts.

It is even easier to get a driver's license in Canada than it is in the United States. A telephone survey of each of the twelve provinces and territories revealed that the only I.D. needed to get a driver's license is a birth certificate and one other piece of I.D. with your name on it. This other piece of I.D. could be anything from club membership cards to baptismal certificates (see chapter on "Supporting I.D.").

The procedure for getting a driver's license in Canada is almost identical to getting one in the U.S. You have to take a written test, a road test and a vision test. The fee in most places is C$9.60. As in the U.S., your license can be suspended if you are convicted of too many moving violations. In most places, the license is made at the examination station and given to you there.

Older Applicants

If you are somewhat older than the average teenager applying for his first driver's license, you should come up with a good story as to why you are applying for one now. For this, you could tell the snoopy clerk: (1) You lived in the big city all your life and relied on public transportation till now; (2) Your parents got divorced when you were young and you lived with your mother in the U.S. till now.

The rest of this chapter contains information and sample formats for each provinces driver's license.

Alberta

This driver's license consists of two separate parts. Part one has the driver's photo and is laminated. Part 2 is on paper stock, unlaminated, and made to be folded in half. In Alberta, driver's licenses are valid for 5 years, expiring on the driver's birthday. The license number is 6 digits, uncoded.

Sample Alberta driver's license, Part 1.

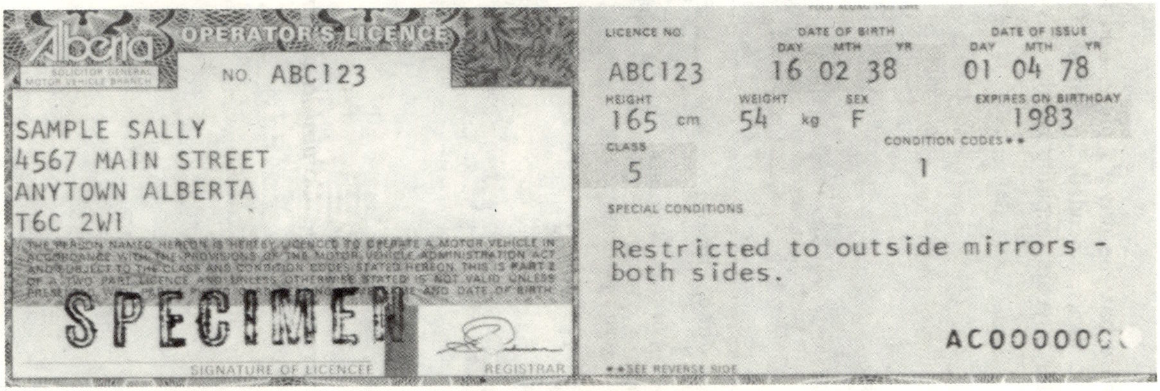

Sample Alberta driver's license, Part 2, shown open.

British Columbia

This driver's license has the driver's photo and is laminated. The license number is 7 digits, uncoded. In British Columbia, driver's licenses are valid for 5 years, expiring on the driver's birthday.

Sample of current British Columbia driver's license.

Manitoba

This driver's license has no photo and is on unlaminated paper stock, made to fold in half. The license number is coded as follows: the first five characters are the first five letters of the driver's last name. The second two characters are the driver's first and second initials. The third two characters are the last two digits of the driver's birth year subtracted from 100. And the last three characters are a check digit and a code for the birth date. In Manitoba, driver's licenses are valid for only one year, and expire on the last day of the driver's birth month.

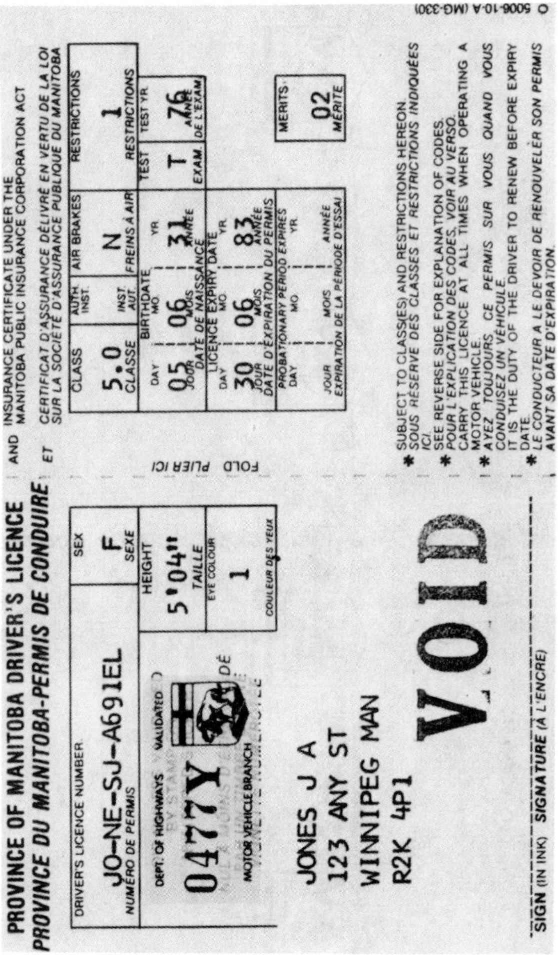

Sample of current Manitoba driver's license.

New Brunswick

This driver's license has no photo and is issued on unlaminated paper stock. The license number contains up to 6 characters, and is not coded. In New Brunswick, driver's licenses are valid up to three years, and expire on the last day of the driver's birth month.

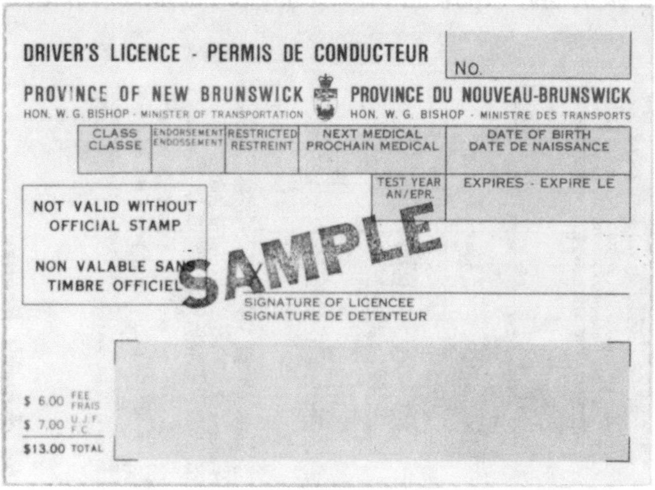

DRIVER'S LICENCE - PERMIS DE CONDUCTEUR

NO.

PROVINCE OF NEW BRUNSWICK PROVINCE DU NOUVEAU-BRUNSWICK

HON. W. G. BISHOP - MINISTER OF TRANSPORTATION HON. W. G. BISHOP - MINISTRE DES TRANSPORTS

CLASS CLASSE	ENDORSEMENT ENDOSSEMENT	RESTRICTED RESTREINT	NEXT MEDICAL PROCHAIN MEDICAL	DATE OF BIRTH DATE DE NAISSANCE

TEST YEAR AN/EPR.

EXPIRES - EXPIRE LE

NOT VALID WITHOUT OFFICIAL STAMP

NON VALABLE SANS TIMBRE OFFICIEL

SAMPLE

SIGNATURE OF LICENCEE
SIGNATURE DE DETENTEUR

$ 6.00 FEE FRAIS
$ 7.00 U.J.F. F.C.
$13.00 TOTAL

Sample of current New Brunswick driver's license.

Newfoundland

This driver's license has no photo, and is issued on unlaminated paper stock made to fold in half. The license number is 5 - 7 computer generated digits, not coded. In Newfoundland, driver's licenses are valid for 36-47 months, and expire on the driver's birth date.

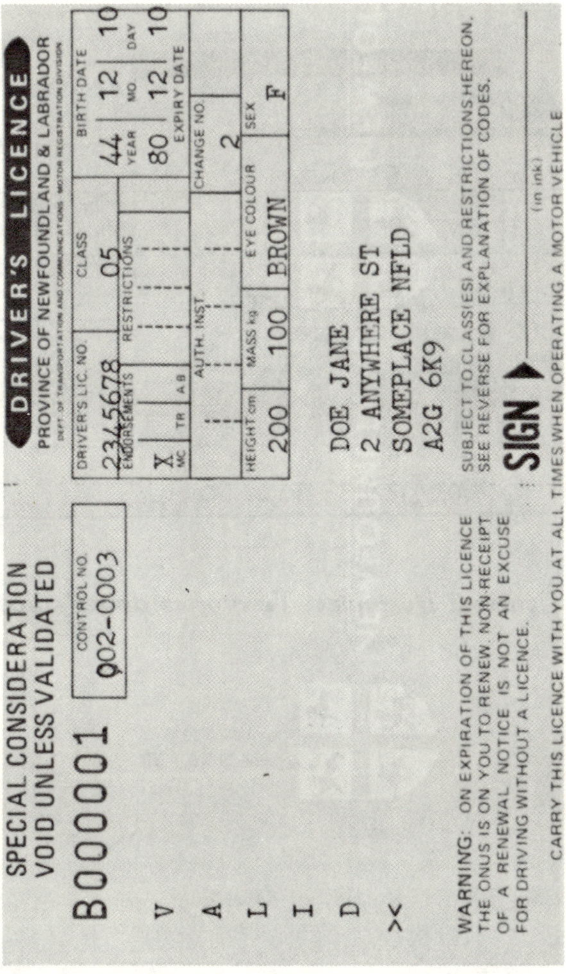

Sample of current Newfoundland driver's license.

Northwest Territories

This driver's license has no picture. It is on unlaminated paper stock. The license number is 5 digits, uncoded. In Northwest Territories, driver's licenses are valid for one year, and always expire on March 31 of the next year.

THIS LICENCE MUST BE CARRIED BY DRIVER
NORTHWEST TERRITORIES
CANADA
1983 MOTOR VEHICLE OPERATOR'S LICENCE
LICENCE NUMBER 00001
CLASS *5 & 6* COND CODE A
FEE PAID $ 5.00
O OR R R
YEAR 19 82
PREVIOUS LICENCE NO. NWT 000
SEX M
HEIGHT 183 cm
EXPIRES 31 MARCH, 1984
NAME
STREET AND NUMBER PUBLIC, John William
000 Robert Crescent
POST OFFICE SETTLEMENT Yellowknife, N.W.T.
DATE OF MEDICAL DAY MONTH YEAR
DATE OF BIRTH DAY 01 MONTH 01 YEAR 45
SIGNATURE OF OPERATOR
X
CANCELLED
ISSUED PURSUANT TO THE VEHICLES ORDINANCE. THIS LICENCE WHEN SIGNED BY THE OPERATOR IS VALID UNTIL MARCH 31ST, 1983 AND MUST BE PRESENTED FOR RENEWAL. APPLICATION FOR 1983 RENEWAL ON REVERSE SIDE.
OFFICE YK
DATED 01/02/83
ISSUER John Doe JD

Sample of current Northwest Territories driver's license.

Nova Scotia

This driver's license has no photo. It is printed on special paper stock of the type used for bank notes, and has latent images for security. The license number is coded with the Soundex system, as explained here: The first 5 characters of the number are the same as the first five letters of the driver's last name. The next six characters are digits, representing the day, month and year of the driver's birth. The final characters are digits representing office codes. In Nova Scotia, driver's licenses are valid for 3 years, expiring on the last day of the birth month of the driver.

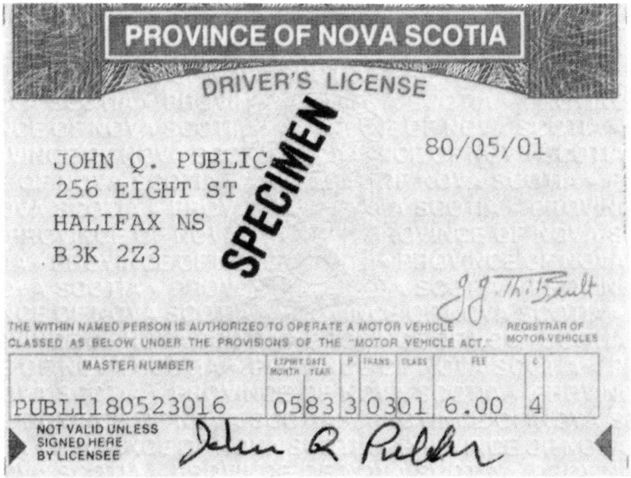

Sample of current Nova Scotia driver's license.

Ontario

This driver's license does not have a photo of the driver. It is issued on unlaminated paper stock. The license number is 15 digits, coded like this: The first character is the same as the first letter of the driver's last name. The next 4 characters are digits coding the last name. The next 4 characters are digits, coded for the first name and middle initial. The next 2 characters are digits, the same as the last 2 digits in the driver's birth year. And the last four digits are the same as the month and day of birth of the driver. Driver's licenses for women have 50 added to the month part of the last 4 digits of the driver's license number. In Ontario, driver's licenses are valid for up to 4 years, and expire on the driver's birthday.

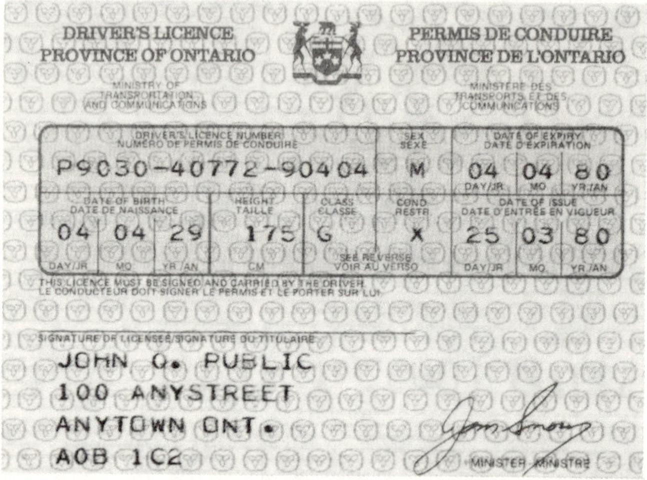
DRIVER'S LICENCE
PROVINCE OF ONTARIO
PERMIS DE CONDUIRE
PROVINCE DE L'ONTARIO
MINISTRY OF TRANSPORTATION AND COMMUNICATIONS
MINISTERE DES TRANSPORTS ET DES COMMUNICATIONS
DRIVER'S LICENCE NUMBER / NUMERO DE PERMIS DE CONDUIRE: P9030-40772-90404
SEX / SEXE: M
DATE OF EXPIRY / DATE D'EXPIRATION: 04 (DAY/JR) 04 (MO) 80 (YR/AN)
DATE OF BIRTH / DATE DE NAISSANCE: 04 (DAY/JR) 04 (MO) 29 (YR/AN)
HEIGHT / TAILLE: 175 (CM)
CLASS / CLASSE: G
COND / RESTR: X
SEE REVERSE / VOIR AU VERSO
DATE OF ISSUE / DATE D'ENTRÉE EN VIGUEUR: 25 (DAY/JR) 03 (MO) 80 (YR/AN)
THIS LICENCE MUST BE SIGNED AND CARRIED BY THE DRIVER
LE CONDUCTEUR DOIT SIGNER LE PERMIS ET LE PORTER SUR LUI
SIGNATURE OF LICENSEE/SIGNATURE DU TITULAIRE
JOHN Q. PUBLIC
100 ANYSTREET
ANYTOWN ONT.
A0B 1C2
MINISTER MINISTRE

Sample of current Ontario driver's license.

Prince Edward Island

This driver's license has the driver's photo, and is laminated. The license number is 12 digits, coded like this: The first 4 digits are the last name coded. The next 6 digits are the same as the day, month and birth year of the driver. The next digit is a code for the driver's sex, with 1 indicating male, and 2 indicating female. The last digit is a check digit. On Prince Edward Island, driver's licenses are valid for 3 years. They may be extended for another 3 years through a validation sticker being attached. All driver's licenses expire on March 31.

Sample of current Prince Edward Island driver's license.

Quebec

This driver's license does not have a photo of the driver. It is issued on unlaminated paper stock. The license number is 11 characters, using the Soundex system, coded like this: The first character is the same as the first letter of the driver's last name. The next four characters are digits coding the last and first name of the driver. The last 6 characters are digits representing the driver's date of birth. In Quebec, driver's licenses are valid for 2 years, and expire on the driver's birthday.

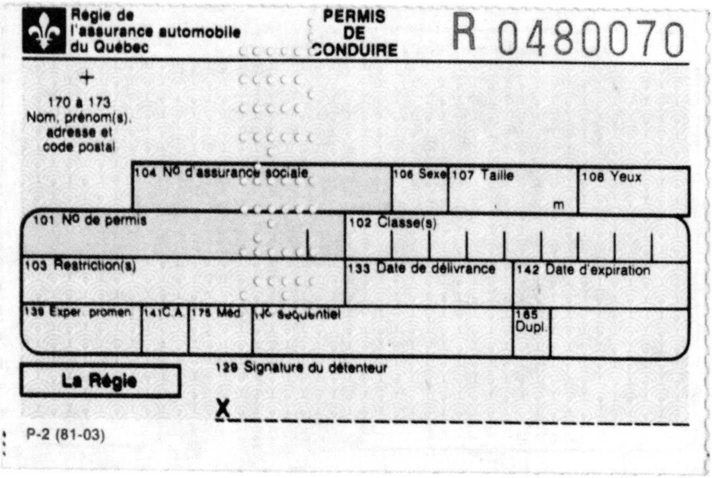

Sample of current Quebec driver's license.

Saskatchewan

This driver's license has no photo, and is issued on unlaminated paper stock. The license number is 8 digits. The first 7 digits are uncoded, with the last one representing an office code. In Saskatchewan, driver's licenses are valid for one year only, and expire on the last day of the driver's birth month.

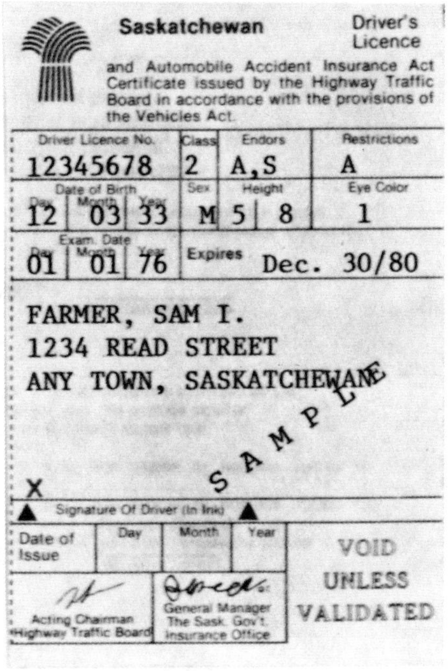

Sample of current Saskatchewan driver's license

Yukon Territory

This driver's license does not have a photo of the driver. It is issued on flexible plastic. The license number is not coded. In Yukon Territory, driver's licenses are valid for 3 years, expiring on the driver's birthday.

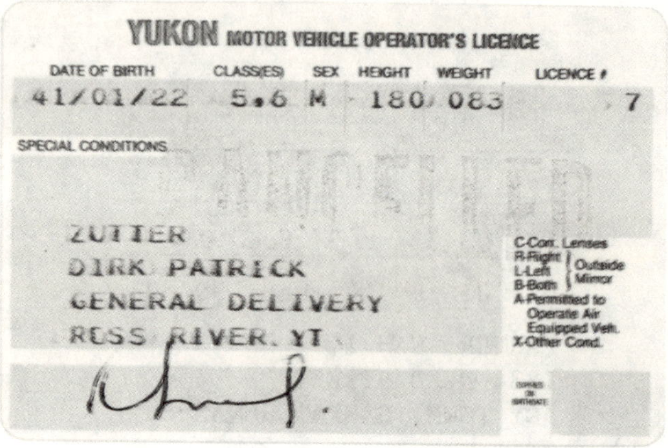

Sample of current Yukon Territory driver's license

How to Get a Canadian Social Insurance Card

It is very easy to get a social insurance card in Canada. Just go into any branch office of the Canadian Employment Commission and apply for it. A telephone survey of three local offices revealed that the only I.D. needed is a Canadian birth certificate and one other piece of I.D. with your name on it. One office stated that telephone bills and rent receipts were acceptable forms of I.D.

The forms you fill out at the local office are sent to a central office in New Brunswick for processing. Your card is mailed to you from there and you should receive it in 3-4 weeks.

If you are over 21, you should come to the office with a good cover story as to what took you so long to apply for a social insurance card. For this, you might say that your mother and father were divorced when you were a child and that you lived in the United States with your mother since that time. Then you could go on to say that you have moved back to Canada because your father's employer has offered you a good job.

Don't worry too much about your cover story. The bureaucrats probably won't ask you anything. The Canadian social insurance card is much easier to get than an American social security card.

How to Get a Canadian Passport

If you are planning on doing any traveling to foreign countries under your new name, you are going to have to get a passport. The only countries that will let you in without one are Mexico and the United States. Even if you aren't going to be traveling abroad, you should still get a passport. They are the most impressive piece of I.D. that you can get. Just looking at one makes you want to stand up and salute.

Procedure for Getting a Canadian Passport

It is a little harder to get a passport in Canada than it is to get one in the U.S.

Passport applications can be obtained from post offices, travel agencies and passport offices. You will need proof of citizenship (a birth certificate) and three identical photographs measuring 2″ x 2¾″ with a signature space at the bottom. The photographer must state where, when and by whom the pictures were taken. He must also certify that it is a true photograph of you.

In addition to the above, a guarantor must sign the passport application and all three photos. The guarantor must have known you personally for at least two years and must be from one of the following groups: doctor, dentist, lawyer, mayor, magistrate, notary public, judge, police officer, or bank officer.

If you don't know a suitable guarantor, you will have to fill out Form PPT 132, "Declaration in Lieu of Guarantor." This form must be filled out before a notary public or commissioner of oaths.

When the passport application is completed, you send it, the birth certificate and, if necessary, Form PPT 132 to the main passport office in Ottawa. Your passport and birth certificate are mailed to you from there and you should receive them within a couple of weeks.

Getting a Canadian Passport While in the United States

Surprisingly, it is easier to get a Canadian passport in the United States than it is in Canada. Simply call up the nearest Canadian consulate or embassy and request that a passport application be mailed to you.

As in Canada, you must have a guarantor for your passport application. The big difference is that in the United States just about anyone can become a notary public. You should be able to find someone to notarize your application. If not, have a friend "become" a notary or even "become" one yourself under a different name.

The rest of the procedure for getting a passport is the same as getting one in Canada, except you have to enclose a photocopy of your U.S. visa or alien registration card. These are available from any American consulate in Canada or at border crossings. You only need to show them a driver's license to get one.

The passport is the I.D. document that is the most difficult to obtain. However, if the application is filled out correctly and your birth certificate is legitimate, you shouldn't have any problems. Millions of Canadians already have one, so don't let the difficult procedure intimidate you. You never know when you might have to leave the country in a hurry, so get a passport as soon as you can.

Other Ways of Getting Fake I.D. in Canada

The infant identity method is by far the best method of getting fake I.D. For the sake of completeness, some other methods will be mentioned here.

Stolen I.D.

One way to get new identification is to steal it. If you lurk in the shadows of a dark alley, sooner or later some poor soul will come walking by. If he looks enough like you, you could waylay him and crack him across the skull with a blunt instrument. You could then go through his pockets and steal his I.D. This method is frowned upon by law enforcement officers and, besides, it lacks class. Obviously, it can not be recommended. Another method of stealing I.D. is to go through the wallets in the Lost and Found departments of theatres, bus stations, department stores, etc., surreptitiously taking what you need.

Counterfeit I.D.

Counterfeiting I.D. is recommended for short-term use only. An advantage of counterfeit I.D. is that it is quick and easy to make, and you can get *exactly* the names you want. But with "infant identity" I.D. so easy to get, counterfeit I.D. should be avoided.

Taking Over the Identity of an Older Dead Person

This method would be the same as the infant identity method, except that instead of using a dead baby, you would obtain the birth certificate of a person who died later in life, and would now be about the age you are. An advantage of this method is that you could easily obtain such documents as college diplomas, etc., that the dead person accumulated during his time alive. Drawbacks are obvious. You might run into someone who knew the person you are claiming to be. You are best off starting from scratch.

Taking Over the Identity of a Living Person

Another method recommended for short-term use only. Con men

sometimes use this method, which simply involves obtaining personal information on some living person, then posing as that person to get copies of all his I.D. One would go to a driver's license office, for example, and say he "lost" his license, and then have them issue him a new one in the dupe's name. One way con men obtain the necessary personal data is to open a fake office and advertise jobs in the newspaper. Anyone applying for the job is required to fill out an Application for Employment, which will contain such questions as: social insurance number, do you have a current passport, what is your mother's maiden name, etc. If you are going to use this method, it would probably be best to take over the identity of a simpleton or bumpkin-type of individual. Such people seldom get into any hot water or do any traveling.

The drawbacks of this method are that you might run into someone who knows the person you are impersonating, or you may even run into that person, himself. The person you are impersonating might be in legal or financial trouble, and might even have problems that make yours look like nothing. Also, if you were caught using a living person's name, that person could sue you for a tidy sum.

Mail Order I.D.

There are dozens of companies who sell all kinds of I.D. cards and documents through the mail. Anything from "driver's licenses" to Ph.D. diplomas complete with transcripts are available. The trouble with this sort of I.D. is that it will not stand up to any sort of in-depth investigation. The most such I.D. should be used for is as supporting I.D. There is an entire book, *I.D. For Sale,* on the subject of what kinds of I.D. you can get through the mail. See Recommended Reading.

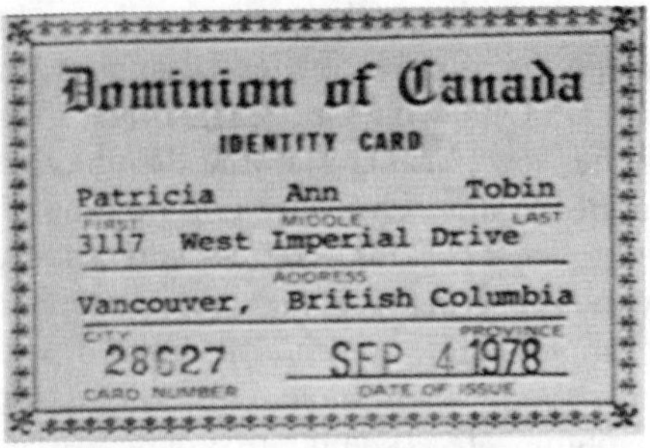

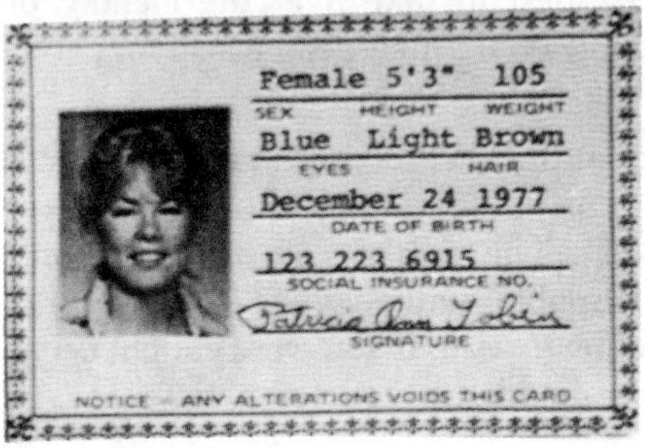

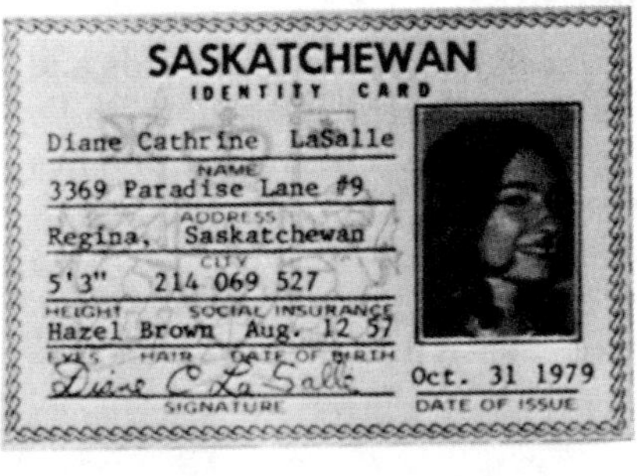

Many types of fake I.D. can be ordered through the mail. Pictured above are four "Canadian I.D. cards" offered by one mail order seller, shown reduced in size.

Mail Drops

Mail forwarding services are private businesses which allow you to use their addresses as your own. Mail addressed to you and received by them will be forwarded to you at whatever address you desire. A mail drop will also forward mail sent by you, under their return address. Thus snoopy people of various kinds will believe you actually live at the address of the mail forwarding service.

The kind of snoopy people we are concerned with in this book are the I.D. bureaucrats. You must have some sort of "address of record" in order for them to issue you the I.D. you want. A mail drop can be used for this.

There are hundreds of mail drops throughout the world, and dozens in Canada. Check the classified ads in such tabloids as *National Enquirer*, and magazines such as *Popular Mechanics, Soldier of Fortune*, and many others. Best of all, obtain a copy of the *Directory of Mail Drops in the United States and Canada*, listed under Recommended Reading.

Getting Fake I.D. in Mexico

The Infant Identity Method works just as well in Mexico as it does in the U.S. and Canada. The procedure is exactly the same.

1. Obtain the birth certificate of a child matching your age and sex.

2. Get some supporting I.D. such as club membership cards, student I.D. cards, etc. (With Mexico becoming predominantly Roman Catholic, a baptismal certificate would be good to have.)

3. Get a driver's license and social insurance card.

4. Get a passport.

Records of births and deaths are kept at the local and state level. On the local level, you can get birth and death records from the office of the civil registrar found in each municipality. Thus in Juarez, Chihuahua, Mexico, you would visit or write to:

Official del Registro Civil
Juarez, Chihuahua
Mexico

Each state also has a similar office where all records of births and deaths that occured within that state are kept. If you were writing for the birth or death certificate of someone from the Yucatan, you would write to:

Archivo General de Gobierno
Palacio de Gobierno
Merida, Yucatan, Mexico

Mexico City has its own office that issues birth and death records. For this city you would write to:

Jefe de la Oficina del Registro
Civil del Distrito Federal
Mexico City, Mexico

The research for finding a dead child matching your age and sex can probably be done in the vital statistics office. If a bureaucrat gives you any problems, just ask if a "special arrangement" (a bribe) can be made. This should immediately solve the problem. The "mordida" is very much alive and well south of the border.

Americans don't have to travel all the way to Mexico to do research. Most Mexican birth and death records are on microfilm at the Latter Day Saints library in Salt Lake City, Utah.

Any Americans trying to get Mexican I.D. should look Hispanic and speak fluent Spanish with no gringo accent. If you are 6′3″, 200 lbs., with blond hair and blue eyes, you're not going to get very far.

Getting a Mexican Passport While in the U.S.

It is fairly easy to obtain a Mexican passport while in the United States. Simply go to the nearest Mexican consulate or embassy and fill out the application. You will need proof of Mexican citizenship (a birth certificate) and two other pieces of I.D. of any kind. Baptismal and marriage certificates are acceptable forms of I.D. The Mexican consulate in Detroit told me that I would need my U.S. alien registration card, but the consulate in Chicago said it wasn't necessary to have one.

You will need three pictures 2″ x 2″ front and side shots. The fee for the passport is U.S. $38.40 for five years or U.S. $14.40 for one year.

It takes about 7 days to receive your passport. You can pick it up at the consulate or it can be mailed to you.

How to Get I.D. in Other Countries

The Infant Identity Method, diagrammed on the next page, will probably work in any free or relatively free country.

I know for a fact that it works well in all British Commonwealth countries (England, Australia, New Zealand, etc.). Reportedly, Australia is the easiest country in the world in which to get fake I.D.

Other countries such as Japan and Sweden keep "social registers" whereby they track people from the cradle to the grave. This would probably make it more difficult to take over the identity of a dead child. However, a little research and creative thought will probably make the basic idea work in these countries, too.

Listed below are the addresses where you would write for birth and death records for most countries in the world. Obviously, not many people would want identification papers from such places as Cuba, Mozambique or Guyana. They are included only for the sake of thoroughness.

Some countries are not listed at all. This is because I was not able to find out where one would write for both birth and death records in these countries.

AFRICA

Algeria
Mayor's office where the event took place.

Burundi
Officer de L'Etat Civil
Bujumbura, Burundi

Cameroon
Mayor's office where the event took place.

Congo
Mayor's office where the event took place.

Dahomey
Mayor's office where the event took place.

Egypt
Public Health Office of the Ministry of Municipal and Rural Affairs where the event took place.

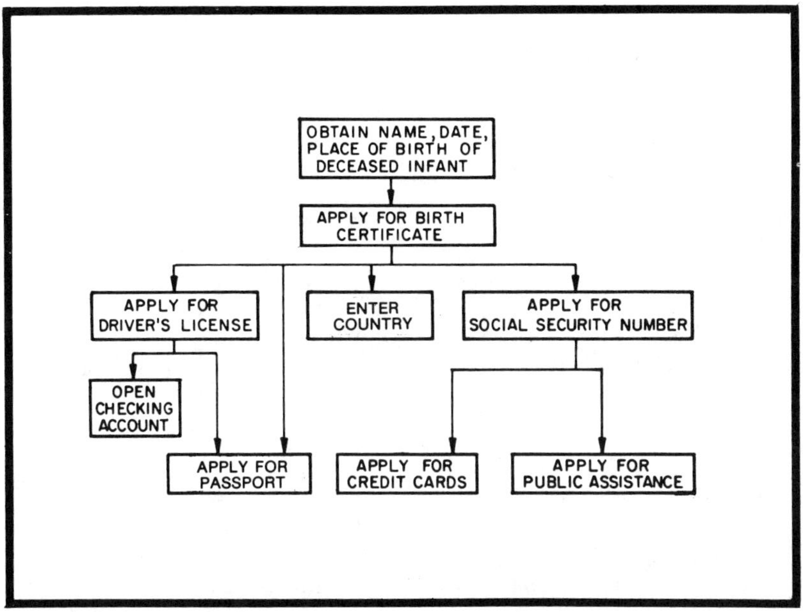

A flowchart demonstrating the steps involved in securing various forms of identification using the Infant Identity Method.

Ethiopia
Residents of Addis Ababa — Municipality of Addis Ababa, Box 356, Menelik II Square, Addis Ababa, Ethiopia.
All other cities — Chief Municipal Authority where the event took place.

Ghana
Registrar General's Office
P.O. Box 118, Accra, Ghana

Ivory Coast
Mayor's office where the event took place.

Kenya
Registrar General's Office
P.O. Box 30031, Nairobi, Kenya

Liberia
Ministry of Public Health and Social Welfare
Monrovia, Liberia

Libya
Cities — Vital statistics office where the event took place.
Outlying areas — District Governor

Malagasy Republic
Chef du district where the event took place.

Malawi
Non-Africans — Registrar General, P.O. Box 1001, Blantyre, Malawi.
Africans — Affidavit of birth by a relative is all that is available.

Mauritania
Registrar General
Sir William Newton Street
Port Louis, Mauritius

Morocco
Bureau de L'Etat Civil
Rabat, Morocco

Mozambique
Conservatoria do Registo Civil where the event took place.

Niger
Presidence de la Republique
Niamey, Niger

Nigeria
Assistant Director of Medical Services
Lagos, Nigeria

Rhodesia ("Zimbabwe")
Deputy Registrar where the event took place.

Senegal
Mayor's office where the event took place.

Sierra Leone
Registrar's Office
Ministry of Health
Oxford Street
Freetown, Sierra Leone

Somalia
Chief Secretary
Mozadishu, Somalia

South Africa
Registrar of Births, Marriages and Deaths
Dept. of the Interior
Private Bag X114
Pretoria, South Africa 0001

Namibia
Same as South Africa.

Sudan
Department of Statistics
Ministry of Social Affairs
Khartoum, Sudan

Swaziland
Registrar of Births, Marriages and Deaths
P.O. Box 19
Mbabane, Swaziland

Tanzania
Registrar General
Dar es Salaam, Tanzania

Togo
Residents of Lome — Etat Civil de Lome
Lome, Togo
Everywhere else — Mayor's office where the event took place.

Tunisia
Municipalite de Tunis
Avenue de Cartage
Tunis, Tunisia

Uganda
Registrar of Births and Deaths
Kampala, Uganda

ASIA

Afganistan
Statistical Bureau of the Ministry of Interior
Kabul, Afganistan

Burma
Registrar of Births, Deaths and Marriages
Office of the Excise Commissioner
Rangoon, Burma

Cyprus
Commisioner of the district where the event took place.

India
State Registrar General of Births, Deaths and Marriages in the state where the event took place.

Indonesia
Kantor Tjatan Sipil in the city where the event took place or
Deportemen Kehakiman R.I.
Biro Research, Penjambon 2
Jakarta, Indonesia

Iraq
Municipal office where the event took place.

Israel
Ministry of Interior
Jerusalem, Israel

Japan
Koseki (family registers are kept in each municipality).

Jordan
Ministry of Health
Amman, Jordan

Korea (North & South)
Family register system similar to Japan.

Laos
Bureau of Vital Statistics where the event took place.

Lebanon
Recensement Estat-Civil in the district where the event took place

Malaysia
Superintendent Registrar of Births and Deaths where the event took place.

Pakistan
Municipal Registrar or Unioun Board where the event took place.

Philippines
Civil registrar where the event took place.

Seychelles
Chief Civil Status Officer
Victoria, Seychelles

Singapore
Registrar of Births, Deaths and Marriages
Singapore, Singapore

Sri Lanka
Dept. of Registrar General
York St.
Colombo 1, Sri Lanka

Syria
Ministry of Interior
Dept. of Civil Status
Damascus, Syria

Thailand
Nai Amphur in the district where the event took place.

Turkey
Population Registration Department where the event took place.

Viet Nam
Administration office where the event took place.

CARIBBEAN

Bahamas
Registrar General
P.O. Box 532
Nassau, Bahamas

Barbados
Registration Office
Coleridge St.
Bridgetown, Barbados

Cuba
Registro Civil where the event took place.

Dominican Republic
Oficina del Estado Civil
Junta Central Electoral
Centro de los Heroes
Santo Domingo, Dominican Republic

Haiti
Officer de L'Etat Civil where the event took place.

Jamaica
Island Record Office
Spanish Town, Jamaica

Trinidad
Registrar General's Office
Port-of-Spain, Trinidad

CENTRAL AMERICA

Nicaragua
Registrar del Estado Civil
Managua, Nicaragua

Panama
Direccion General del Registro Civil
Apartado 5281
Panama 5, Republica de Panama

El Salvador
Alcaldias office where the event took place.

Costa Rica
Registro Central del Estado Civil
San Jose, Costa Rica

Guatemala
Registro Civil where the event took place.

Honduras
Civil Registry where the event took place.

SOUTH AMERICA

Argentina
Registro Civil where the event took place.

Bolivia
Registro Civil in the district where the event took place or General del Registro Civil
La Paz, Bolivia

Brazil
Registro Civil where the event took place.

Chile
Direccion General del Registro Civil e Identificacion
Santiago, Chile

Columbia
Notario Publico or municipal authority where the event took place.

Ecuador
Civil Registrar where the event took place or Direccion General del Registro Civil
Quito, Ecuador

French Guiana
Mayor's office where the event took place.

Guyana
General Register Office
GPO Building
Georgetown, Guyana

Peru
Consejo Provincial or Consejo Distrital where the event took place.

Uruguay
Juez de Paz where the event took place.

Venezuela
Jefe Civil in the district where thé event took place or Consejo Municipal in the city where the event took place.

AUSTRALIA

New South Wales
The Registrar-General
Prince Albert Road
2000 Sydney
New South Wales, Australia

Queensland
The Registrar General
Treasury Building
400 Brisbane, B7
Queensland, Australia

South Australia
The Principal Registrar
Box 1351 H GPO
5001 Adelaide
South Australia, Australia

Tasmania
The Registrar General
Box 875 GPOJ
7001 Hobart
Tasmania, Australia

Victoria
Government Statistics
295 Queen St.
300 Melbourne, Victoria
Australia

Western Australia
The Registrar General
Oakleigh Bldg.
22 St. George's Terrace
6000 Perth
Western Australia, Australia

Northern Territory
Registrar-General
P.O. Box 367
5794 Darwin
Northern Territory, Australia

Australian Capital Territory
The Registrar General
P.O. Box 1515
Canberra City, Australian Capital
Territory 2600, Australia

PACIFIC ISLANDS

Fiji
Registrar General
Suva, Fiji

New Zealand
Registrar General
P.O. Box 5023
Lambton Quay
Wellington 1, New Zealand

Tonga
Registrar of the Supreme Court
Naku'alofa, Tonga

EUROPE

Andorra
Mayor's office where the event took place.

Austria
Rectory of the parish where the event took place.

Belgium
Greffes des Tribunaux de
Premiere Instance
Brussels, Belgium

Bulgaria
District People's Council where the event took place.

Czechoslovakia
Local National Committee where the event took place.

Denmark
Rigsarkivet
9 Rigsdagsgarden
Copenhagen K Denmark

France
Greffe de Tribunaux d'Instance
Paris, France

Germany (West)
Local Standesamt where the event took place

Greece
Mayor's office in all cities except Athens, Piraeus, and Saloniki. These cities have "Special Registration Bureaus."

Hungary
Registry office where the event took place.

Iceland
Local clergy where the event took place.

Ireland
General Registrar of Births, Deaths and Marriages
Custom House
Dublin 1, Ireland

Italy
Vital Statistics Office where the event took place.

Lichtenstein
Parsonage where the event took place.

Luxembourg
Greffes des Tribunaux
Luxembourg, Luxembourg

Malta
Directory of the Public Registry Office
L'Insinua, Merchants Street
Valleta, Malta

Monaco
Bureau de L'Etat-Civil
Mairie de Monaco
Principaute de Monaco

Netherlands
Civil Registrar's Office of the Burgomaster where the event took place

Norway
Parish where the event took place.

Poland
Local vital statistics office where the event took place.

Portugal
Office of the civil registrar where the event took place.

Rumania
Oficiul Starii Civile
Sfatul Popular
Bucharest, Rumania

Spain
Municipal Court where the event took place.

Sweden
Parish office where the event took place.

Switzerland
French-speaking Switzerland:
Officer de L'Etat Civil where the event took place.
German-speaking Switzerland:
Zivilstandbeamter where the event took place.
Italian-speaking Switzerland:
Ufficiale della Stato Civale where the event took place.

Yugoslavia
Peoples Committee where the event took place.

United Kingdom
General Register Office
St. Catherine's House
10 Kingsway
London WC2B 6JP, England

Staying Free

Once you have changed your name and obtained new identification papers, it will be almost impossible for a government or private investigator to find you.

Traditional methods of locating "missing persons" (driver's licenses, credit checks, criss-cross directories, etc.) are of no value when the person being sought has changed his name.

Assuming that you are not going to do anything stupid, the only way an investigator can find you is through a friend or a relative who knows where you are.

If you are on the run from the law, it would probably be best not to reveal your new name and location to friends and relatives. If you must make contact with people, call them from a pay phone far away from your new location and do not call collect. It's wise to assume that their phone is tapped, so don't make any statements that would give you away.

If they need to get in touch with you, have them place a pre-arranged coded ad in a weekly newspaper such as the *National Enquirer.*

You should also forget about continuing any distinctive occupations or hobbies you might have such as raising Dobermans or even visiting race tracks.

If you are on the run from creditors, an ex-spouse, etc., you need not go to such extremes. You can tell *trusted* friends and relatives your new name and location provided that the following precautions are taken:

1. Warn your friends and relatives to be alert for ruses and tricks perpetrated by people looking for you. People might call or visit claiming to be "old friends" wanting to get in touch with you. "Doctors" might call claiming they need to get in touch with you about an "emergency" of some sort. The ruse or trick could be anything imaginable, so make sure that those who know your new name and location are on guard.

2. Tell friends and relatives never to call you from their home phone. Also never call them collect. A good private operator (P.I., repo-man,

skip-tracer, etc.) can get the phone records of anybody in the country within twenty minutes. (See my books *How to Find Missing Persons*, volumes 1 and 2, in the Recommended Reading section.)

3. Under a different name than your alias, open an account with a mail-forwarding service in a different country from where you live. Mail forwarding services in the United States are immune from court orders in Canada and vice versa. Again, warn the mail forwarding service owner about ruses and tricks.

Keeping the Hounds off Your Trail

Here are a few things you can do to make life miserable for anyone trying to track you down:

1. Leave travel brochures for a vacation area in the trash at your old residence. The vacation area should be one that you are unlikely to visit in the near future. An investigator finding such a "clue" might be misled into thinking you are headed for the area shown in the brochure.

2. Any credit cards that you might have under your old name should be left in a bus station in a large city. Such bus stations are infested with low-life characters of all kinds and you can be sure that your credit cards will be given a good workout all over the country. This trick will confuse any investigator who obtains your credit card records.

3. File a change of address form with your local post office and have your mail forwarded to someone with a similar name to yours. The people who are trying to find you will face a heavy lawsuit if they harass this person in any way. You can find people with similar names to yours by going through telephone directories.

4. After you are gone for a while, have relatives make phone calls to a low class bar in a city far away from where you actually live. If an investigator should obtain their phone records he might think you hang out at that bar.

5. Leave a suicide note on the Golden Gate or other large bridge, stating that you have jumped off. Have a friend call the police and say that he saw someone of your description take the big dive.

Famous Last Words

As this work concludes, it becomes obvious that "I.D." is nothing more than bureaucratic paper. "If you give the bureaucrats the paper they want, they will give you the paper you want" is how one noted authority described the situation.

In the next few years, technology will bring us new kinds of bureaucratic paper. Injectable I.D., computer implants, and hand scan machines are already in use today. Politicians and people of their ilk will not be able to resist forcing these technologies upon us. It behooves all freedom seekers to keep abreast of these new I.D. technologies and develop countermeasures to them. The world that George Orwell warned us about in his novel *1984* is here.

Appendix I

A Survey of Foreign National Systems for Personal Identification

Contents

SECTION I

INTRODUCTION

Purpose

The Federal Advisory Committee on False Identification (FACFI) is investigating the problem of false identification in commission of criminal acts. As a part of this investigation this report documents the results of a survey of the related experience of various foreign countries. The interest of the U.S. Government in this matter is in the following two general areas:

1. Many foreign countries have used advanced techniques of personal identification for many years and the U.S. can, therefore, profit by their experience.

2. Some U.S. problems, such as illegal immigration and drug smuggling, involve falsification of foreign documents. The U.S., therefore, has need to know about foreign personal identification procedures to effectively combat the use of such false documents.

This report is intended to provide a general appreciation of the false identification problems in foreign countries; however, since it is based on limited data, it should not be considered a reference document.

Sources of Data

The principal sources of information used in this report are surveys made by the U.S. State Department through embassy channels and by the International Criminal Police Organization (INTERPOL).* The INTERPOL survey covered twenty-five countries of which sixteen replied. The State Department survey[1] covered fourteen countries of which twelve replied. A total of thirty countries were included in these surveys. Countries providing useful information to the INTERPOL survey[2] included: Australia, Austria, Bermuda, Denmark, Egypt, France, West Germany, Jamaica, Japan, the Netherlands, Peru, Spain, and the United Kingdom. Useful inputs to the State Department survey were provided by Argentina, Brazil, Colombia, France, West Germany, Greece, Italy, Japan, Romania, Sweden and the United Kingdom.

The general response to these surveys was excellent considering that this was an initial effort. Specific questions on identification procedures, laws, identity documents used, etc. were responded to in a useful manner by a large portion of the addressees. More general

*The questions asked in these surveys are shown in Attachments A and B.

questions involving such considerations as social cost of false identification were not consistently answered. There were some indications of a lack of appreciation for or understanding of the problem of false identification by some of the countries responding.

The results of these surveys were supplemented to the extent possible from other sources. The most useful of these other sources was the report of the International Symposium on Automation of Population Register Systems held in Jerusalem, Israel, 25-28 September 1967, and sponsored by the International Federation for Information Processing.[3] This report contained useful information on actual or planned population register systems in Denmark, Finland, West Germany, India, Israel, Italy, the Netherlands, Norway, Sweden and Switzerland.

From all sources, significant information was received pertinent to twenty-five countries.

SECTION II

FALSE ID PROBLEMS IN OTHER LANDS

Common Personal Identification Documents

The most common identification document used in the countries surveyed is a national identity card (commonly referred to as a national identification document or national ID). Fifteen out of the twenty-one countries about which we have positive information use such a document. One (Greece) has a police identity document which is approximately equivalent. Peru is planning to establish a national ID. All countries have passports; however, these are not normally used for identification purposes within the country of issue. All countries issue drivers licenses. In addition, police and military identification cards, health insurance cards, company identification cards, social security cards, selective service cards, voter and tax registration cards are used in varying degrees as a means of identification in the countries surveyed.

In countries which have national IDs, this is the normal means of identification. Where no such document exists, there is a tendency for documents issued for other purposes to be used as a substitute for it. In the United Kingdom, the National Health Insurance card, and in Switzerland the national social insurance card performs this function to a limited extent.

The cards used for personal identification are supported by personal or family records and by application procedures which are part of the identification process. Application procedures include use of photographs and/or fingerprints, personal questionnaires, certificates from officials and citizens, employers or use of other supportive documentation. The most common supportive documents used are birth and marriage certificates. The value of an identification document as a means of providing assurance that the bearer is correctly identified is derived from the total process involved in issuing such documents and not solely on any inherent characteristics associated with the document per se. Table I lists the supporting documentation and procedures involved in the issuance of a representative cross section of identity documents from various countries.

The existence of considerable numbers of resident aliens among the population poses a special problem of personal identification. For very short-term visits (less than 2 months) the passport or visa issued by their country of citizenship is normally sufficient identification. National identity documents issued by the countries of the European Economic Community are also commonly recognized by all members of that community. For longer periods of residence some other form

TABLE I

DOCUMENTS AND PROCEDURES USED TO OBTAIN IDENTITY DOCUMENTS

COUNTRY	DOCUMENTS OBTAINED	SUPPORTING DOCUMENTS USED									PROCEDURES USED				SUPPORTING STATEMENTS OR CERTIFICATES						ISSUED BY	
		National ID Card	Passports	Drivers License	Birth Certificate	Marriage Certificate	Military Records	Family Register	Employer ID Card	Other Documents	Fingerprints	Photographs	Mail Notification to Address of Record	Personal Questionnaire	Employer Statement	Citizens Certificate	Officials Certificate	Certificate of Residence	Certificates of Citizenship	Voter Registration	Local Police	Other Local Authorities
AUSTRALIA	Passport				X	X						X			X	X	X		X			X
BRAZIL	National ID Card				X	X				X	X	X		X							X	
DENMARK	Passport			X	X		X			X				X		X					X	
EGYPT	National ID Card				X										X	X				X		
	Passport				X										X					X		
FRANCE	National ID Card				X	X		X				X									X	
	Passport	X	X					X				X									X	
	Drivers License											X						X			X	
GERMANY	Passport	X			X	X						X		X								X
	National ID Card				X	X						X		X								X
	Drivers License	X	X		X																	X
GREECE	Police ID				X						X	X		X		X					X	
JAPAN	Passport			X				X	X	X			X									
	Drivers License									X		X									X	
SPAIN	National ID Card				X			X			X	X		X								
	Passport	X				X		X			X	X					X					
	Drivers License	X										X				X	X					
SWEDEN	National ID Card	X		X					X	X	X	X					X					X
UNITED KINGDOM												X					X					
KINGDOM	Passport											X					X					
NETHERLANDS	Passport		X										X	X								X
COLOMBIA	National ID Card					X					X	X										

of temporary or permanent identification is commonly required. Brazil and Argentina issue identity cards to resident aliens which are similar to those used by citizens. Germany and Greece use residence permits. Japan requires a certificate of alien registration. In the United Kingdom national passports are used by resident, long-term aliens who are citizens of the British Commonwealth. Those who are citizens of the European Economic Community are issued a resident's permit. Other aliens in permanent residence must have a police registration certificate. Other countries probably use similar documents for identification of aliens, but did not indicate these in the survey.

Nature and Scope of False Identification

The information received from survey respondents on the nature and scope of the false identification problem was in most cases very limited. The United Kingdom, however, provided a detailed listing of uses of documents for false identity. Birth certificates, passports, social security cards, drivers licenses, immigration, nationality and registration certificates, credit cards and examination certificates were frequently used to establish a false identity. False documents were used in illegal immigration (including that of fugitive offenders), to obtain goods fraudulently, to drive illegally, to obtain employment for which the applicant was not qualified and for general identification purposes. Argentina cited the use of illegal certificates to establish U. S. citizenship, and use of lost passports for drug trafficking, smuggling, etc. Australia and Japan cited the fraudulent obtaining of passports. Several countries cited problems related to foreigners using false foreign drivers licenses and other problems involving aliens as a source of false identification problems.

The extent of the problem of false identity perceived by countries responding to our surveys can be categorized as follows:

I. Significant Problems Exist

Australia, Colombia, United Kingdom

II. Some Problems Exist

Argentina, Egypt, France, West Germany, Peru, Sweden

III. No Significant Problems Exist

Denmark, Japan, the Netherlands, Romania, Spain

For the other countries included in the data base, there was insufficient information on which to make a judgment.

An attempt was made to correlate the reported extent of the problem of misuse of identity documents with the International Crime

Statistics by INTERPOL for the years 1969-1970 and 1971-1972. This attempt was unsuccessful in that statistics in these documents cover very broad categories of crimes only and none of these could be directly associated with misuse of identity documents.

False ID and the Law

Ten countries (Argentina, Australia, Brazil, Colombia, France, Germany, Greece, Japan, Spain and Sweden) supplied responses to our queries as to legal penalties for use of documents for false identification.

The applicable provisions of the laws provided by the above ten countries have been summarized in Table II. This table provides a comparative picture of the legal constraints within these countries and, to the extent that these countries are typical, of the worldwide variation in legal penalties for use of documents to establish false identity.

The French laws are among the most complete; they cover all significant documents and the most significant ways in which crimes involving false identification could be committed. An extract of these laws has, therefore, been included as Attachment C to this report. The laws of Brazil and Germany are very similar to those of France. Japanese laws are also very thorough; however, the use of false identification documents (as contrasted to their production) does not appear to be included. Argentina, Colombia, Greece, Spain and Sweden provide substantial penalties; however, the coverage is not as comprehensive as for the French laws. All of these countries have laws which could be real deterrents to false identification. In contrast, the Australian laws cover only limited aspects of the problem and do not appear to be a significant deterrent.

Other countries in the data base may have similar laws, but did not describe them. Crimes involving misuse of identity documents may also be covered by more general laws covering the specific crimes committed. For example, an individual who uses illegally obtained documents in the process of committing embezzlement or fraud may be prosecuted for embezzlement or fraud rather than the associated act of false identification. The existence of specific laws against the creation and use of false identity documents such as those listed in Table II provides a significant deterrent even in cases in which no other serious crime was involved.

TABLE II

SUMMARY OF LAWS ON MISUSE OF IDENTITY DOCUMENTS

COUNTRY	AUSTRALIA	FRANCE	GREECE	JAPAN	SPAIN
IDENTITY DOCUMENTS COVERED	Passports	Permits, Certificates, Memorandum books, Cards, Reports, Receipts, Passports, Laisser-passer, etc.	Documents, Police ID	(a) Official Documents, (b) Private Documents, (c) Official Seals/Signatures, (d) Private Seals/Signatures	Documents, certificates
ACTS PUNISHABLE BY LAWS					
(a) Counterfeits, forges, falsifies, alters document		6 mo.-1 yr. imprisonment 1500-15,000 Frs. fine 5-10 yrs. loss of civil rights	At least 3 mo. imprisonment *Up to 10 yr. incarceration	*(a)1-10 yr (b)3mo.-5 yr. **(a)Up to 3 yr or 300 yen fine **(b)Up to 1 yr or 100 yen fine (c)3 mo-5 yr (d)Up to 3 yr	Major detention
(b) Issues/utters false document (official or public servant)		1-4 yr imprisonment 1500-15,000 Frs. Fine 5-10 yr. loss of civil rights -			
(c) Uses false or obsolete document		Same as (a) above	Same as (a) above		Major detention 5,000-10,000 pesetas fine
(d) Obtains document using false information	50 pounds or 3 mo. imprisonment	3 mo-2 yr imprisonment 500-5000 Frs. fine		*(a)Up to 5 yr or 1000 yen fine **(a)Up to 1 yr or 300 yen fine	
(e) Uses document obtained using false information		Same as above			
(f) Drafts false document				(a) and (b) Same as (a) above	
(g) Fails to return invalid document or one obtained using false information	50 pounds or 3 mo. imprisonment				
(h) Attempts to commit above acts		Same as for act attempted		Same as for act attempted *Involving misuse of Seals or Signatures **Not involving misuse of Seals or Signatures	

TABLE II (Concluded)

ACTS PUNISHABLE BY LAWS

COUNTRY	ARGENTINA	BRAZIL	GERMANY	SWEDEN	COLOMBIA
IDENTITY DOCUMENTS COVERED	National ID Card All documents (forgery)	All identity documents	Birth Certificates, Drivers Licenses, Other Identity Documents	All official records or documents submitted as a means of establishing identity	Documents, Passports, National ID
(a) Counterfeits, forges, falsifies, alters document	6 mo.-2 yr. imprisonment	2-6 yr imprisonment Fine up to $1.00 U.S.	Up to 5 yr. imprisenment	Up to 2 yr. imprisonment	
(b) Issues/Utters false document (official or public servant)		1-5 yr. imprisonment	Up to 5 yr. imprisonment or fine		6 mo.-3 yr. imprisonment, Fine, Job suspension
(c) Uses false or obsolete document	2 yr. up imprisonment	2-6 yr. imprisonment	Up to 1 yr. imprisonment or fine	Up to 2 yr. imprisonment	3-10 yr. imprisonment Up to $1800 fine
(d) Obtains document using false information		1-5 yr. imprisonment Fine up to $1.00 U.S.	Up to 1 yr. imprisonment 3 mo.-5 yr. (aggravated)	Up to 2 yr. imprisonment	3-10 yr. imprisonment Up to $1800 fine
(e) Uses document obtained using false information	2 yr. up imprisonment	1-5 yr. imprisonment Fine up to $1.00 U.S.	Up to 1 yer. imprisonment 3 mo.-5 yr. (aggravated)		
(f) Drafts false documents					(Penalties are not normally enforced)
(g) Fails to return invalid document or one obtained using false information					
(h) Attempts to commit above acts					
(i) Use of false name by alien		1-3 yr. imprisonment. Fine up to $1.00 U.S.			

SECTION III

METHODS OF PERSONAL IDENTIFICATION

Personal identification systems used in foreign countries consist of a collection of components with various degrees of national control. The effectiveness of these systems depends both upon the design of these components and how well the components are coordinated within the complete system. The most complete systems contain the following major components:

a. National identity document or equivalent.
b. Family or personal records.
c. Population register.

We will discuss each of these components in turn below. In Section IV the personal identification systems of selected countries are described on an integrated basis.

a. National Identity Document

In most of the countries surveyed, the national ID is the primary means of identification. It is normally a pocket-sized, folding card which contains essential information required for personal identification. This information consists as a minimum of name, date of birth (birth number may be included in some countries), address, and identification document number. In some countries additional information such as personal characteristics (height, weight, color of eyes and hair, blood group, occupation, religion, name of father, mother and spouse) may be added. Specific detailed information was obtained on six National ID's. All of these required signatures and photographs and four of these six documents contained fingerprints. Spain employs a unique technique of placing the fingerprints half on and half off the photograph, thereby making it difficult to substitute photographs without detection. Various techniques of fabrication are known to be used to make alteration or forgery more difficult; however, very little specific information on this subject has been made available.

In most countries the national identity document must be carried at all times; however, this is not universal and in at least one country (West Germany) the national identity document is not normally carried on a day-to-day basis.

The most important item on this document is the identifying number. This number is unique and carefully controlled. Through the use of this number, the personal records kept on the population can be accessed. For this reason, it is possible in many countries through the use of this number alone to provide reasonable verification that an individual is the person he claims to be, and it may also be relatively easy to detect a false document by its incorrect number.

b. Family or Personal Records

Three of the countries surveyed (France, Japan and Spain) maintain a system of family records in which changes in the personal status of all members of the family (births, deaths, marriages, divorce, adoption, etc.) are recorded. These records are historically well established and are the basic reference in establishing a person's identity. They are, for example, used as a required supporting document for issuance of national identity documents or passports in these countries. The existence of these carefully maintained family records provides a good assurance that the country's population is accurately and correctly identified and a positive basis for a personal identification program.

c. Population Register

Many countries have well established population registration systems. The use of such systems is widespread in Western Europe and especially in Scandinavia and the Netherlands. The Swedish population register system is 300 years old. The Netherlands' population register system originated with a Royal Decree in 1849. Other systems have been in use for several decades.

These population registration systems have historically been developed in response to fundamental long-standing needs of governments for information on inhabitants in much the same way as, for example, William the Conqueror felt required to make the population survey of England which resulted in the famous Doomsday Books in the eleventh century. The principal application for population register systems is for statistical purposes (including census data). For an established system the creation of new sub-registers for specialized purposes is relatively easy and inexpensive (especially in highly automated systems) and the number of applications tend to multiply. A review of eight population register systems identified the following uses: statistics, census, voting rolls, tax records, police records, criminal records, military records, health insurance, national insurance, public health programs, educational programs, national pensions, social security, church records, welfare, civil servant registers, federal payrolls, and public utilities.

The ability to identify individuals is a necessary pre-requisite and by-product of the existence of personal register systems. Those countries which have a well organized population registration system consistently claim that they have minimal problems of misuse of identity documents and in many cases give primary credit to these systems for that condition.

In a sophisticated system, population registers operate as portions of an overall personal register system consisting of the following general components:

1. A personal and/or family record (see Section IIIb).
2. A personal identity card or as a minimum a personal number uniquely identifying every registered person in the country (see Section IIIa).
3. Local population registers containing general information on inhabitants of a town, parish, or other administrative sub-unit.
4. A central population register containing minimal information on each registered individual in the country.
5. Sub-registers or associated registers dedicated to specific applications (taxation, motor vehicles, etc.).
6. Procedures for making inputs into and obtaining outputs from the system.

All of these components are tied together by the personal number (generally the same number used in the national identity document).

Although the manner of operation of population registers can vary extensively, the most common procedure is to establish a population register at the local government level which contains a reasonably detailed amount of information on each individual and a consolidated but somewhat abbreviated record covering all residents at a central office in each country. Generally, the local registers are under the control of local administrative officials, who may be clergy acting in a civil capacity, tax officials, or police.

The operation of the central registers is a responsibility of a central bureau of statistics or some similar agency. The amount of information in the local population registers varies. In an automated system one data card per individual is normally required. At the central register either a duplicate of this card or a simplified card containing only identifying information may be used. The data card used with the Danish population register system contains all the information listed for the national identity document described in Section IIIa plus information on pensions, health insurance, conscription status, occupation, tax and election numbers, declaration of incapacity and several data fields allocated to changes in status, local use, etc.

Both the local and central registers are interconnected with a series of other registers in which detailed information within a specialized area of interest is stored. Sensitive information which should not be available for general use is normally confined to these specialized registers. The maximum number of specialized registers identified as being associated with a population register system for the countries surveyed was ten (in Finland). There is regular feedback between these registers and the population registers in order to keep all of them up-to-date. Regular inputs are also obtained from the offices of records for birth, marriage and death certificates, immigration and emigration, census, taxes, voting, etc. Population registers are routinely updated on a weekly or monthly basis to reflect any change in status or address of covered personnel. This systematic updating and routine interaction with all the official actions affecting a person's status makes it very difficult for an error in personal identification to remain undetected for any length of time.

There are a number of problems that a population register system must solve to be effective. The most common problems are:

a. Obtaining and maintaining a single list of person numbers corresponding to all covered individuals,
b. Maintaining good address locations,
c. Security of information.

The problem of maintaining a complete, accurate person list is especially important in initiating a personal registration system. It is inherently interrelated to the maintaining of addresses. People may have multiple residences or move without notification. For a personal register system to work, each individual must be associated with a single precise location. He must not change that location without appropriate action with respect to the personal register system. For this reason Finland and Sweden tie their population register system into a land (real estate) register. To assure a single listing for all registrants, it is necessary to keep track of persons who are transients in the system. Separate sub-registers are often maintained for persons who have died, emigrated, are listed as missing, etc.

A census is a good means of correcting a population list. Israel, by correlating its population registers with the 1961 census, reduced incorrect listings from approximately 25% to around 0.5%.

Countries with population registration systems have a keen awareness of the necessity to preserve personal security and privacy. The most common actions taken are to limit the amount of information in the central registers and to maintain the most sensitive information (criminal records, etc.) in related files which are not for public use. Fairly strong controls are generally maintained to insure that only limited information (name, address) is made available to private parties. Potential abuse of registration systems by government officials and employees is controlled by careful supervision and imposing substantial legal penalties for violations of trust. The fact that these measures for assuring security of information can be successful is evidenced by the rapid growth of personal registration systems right after World War II in three countries which had recently suffered through occupation by a foreign power (Finland, Norway, the Netherlands). Under the circumstances one would expect the population to be suspicious of any personal identification system that displayed a vulnerability to government abuse.

It is worthy of note that the three problems associated with population registers must also be solved by any personal identification system.

d. Other Methods of Identification

Countries which have either a national identification document, a family record or a population registration system tend to place primary reliance on them for personal identification. The majority of the countries included in the data base are in this category. For those countries which do not have an official legal personal identification system a variety of documents may be used to establish identity. The most frequently used documents are drivers licenses, passports, bank cards, health insurance or social security cards. These same documents may be used as supplemental means of identification in countries having formal identification systems. The design and credibility of these documents varies widely. A drivers license, for example, can be a reliable means of identification in countries such as Japan or Spain, which rigidly control its issuance and manufacture. In others, it is no more reliable than in the U.S.

Documents used for registration of aliens tend to be similar in design and utilization to comparable ones used by citizens. The alien residence permit used in Greece and the temporary resident's identity card in Brazil resemble very closely the police or national identification card used for citizens.

The procedures which govern application, investigation and issuance of identity documents are an essential element in the personal identification process. These procedures are closely associated with the concept of a legal domicile. In countries with formal personal registration systems every individual has a single legal residence and a location where his personal records are kept. These may or may not be the same; however, in all cases these locations are a part of the personal records, are unambiguous and are not changed without formal procedures. All applications for identity documents are accompanied by some statement of personal history. Matching this personal history and the physical characteristics of the individual with the information in personal or family registers provides a relatively strong assurance that the applicant has identified himself correctly. Statements or certificates from knowledgeable citizens or local officials are also used to support the application. In the Netherlands and Japan (and possibly other countries) a notification to pick up his completed identity document is mailed to the applicant at his established legal residence as shown in the personal records. This makes it difficult for someone who does not live at that residence to falsely obtain such documents.

The degree of confidence in the authenticity of personal identification documents is derived from the combination of supporting documentation, investigative procedures and personal records. Table I (on page 4) gives an overview of the documentation and procedures used to obtain selected identity documents.

SECTION IV

IDENTITY SYSTEMS OF REPRESENTATIVE COUNTRIES

In this section we discuss identity systems used in selected countries in relation to the problem of false identification. These countries have been selected to provide a representative cross-section of the types of identification systems used. The systems surveyed fall in the following categories:

(a) Highly centralized systems using national identity documents and sophisticated population register systems. Denmark, the Netherlands, Norway, Sweden, and Finland are considered to be in this category.

(b) Systems in which much authority is delegated to the lower government levels and there is no legally recognized identity document or integrated population system. (Australia and the United Kingdom are in this category.)

(c) Systems which are at various levels of centralization in between the two extremes described above. All of the other countries in the data base are in this category.

Sweden has been selected as representative of the highly centralized systems. The United Kingdom is representative of the less highly organized systems. West Germany represents an intermediate level of centralization. Japan has a unique system which is of interest. Brazil has been selected as one of the more highly developed Latin American countries.

Sweden

Sweden, a country of 8 million people, is divided into 25 provinces (or counties), communes and parishes. It has a system of population registers which is 300 years old and is apparently well accepted because it was considered essential for providing fair income taxation, maintaining accurate election rolls, etc. Another contributing factor may be that Sweden, like other Scandinavian countries has a limited number of surnames and Swedish names do not by themselves provide adequate identification. The heart of this system is the Civic Registration Office, maintained in each parish by the parish vicar in his civil capacity as a census official. This dual role for church officials is not unusual in countries which, like Sweden, have national churches. At the Civic Registration Office a basic record is kept for each person in the parish (including immigrants and aliens) from birth until death.

Each person's basic record is kept on a separate document containing name, data and place of birth, nationality, parent's name, civil status, name of husband or wife and children, and other pertinent information on his status which has administrative or legal significance. This information is filed by a ten-digit civic registration number containing in its internal design information on date of birth, province of birth, sex and sequence number. This number is unique and will stay with the person it identifies throughout his life.

Consolidated population registers are maintained by counties and a Central Population Register is maintained by the National Board of Civic Registration and Tax Collection. The system is largely automated. It is interconnected with other registers devoted to motor vehicles, drivers licenses, military personnel, and land (real estate).

All births, marriages, deaths, divorces and name changes are registered with the Civic Registration Office. Changes of residence must be sent to the parish office within two weeks. In addition, landlords, the post office, hospitals (births and deaths), courts and social security agencies routinely submit changes of status within their jurisdiction to the Civic Registration Office. The entire system is updated on a weekly basis. There is an annual registration as of 1 November each year, at which time the entire population register is updated and the legal residence of individuals is established for the following year.

In Sweden two types of documents are commonly used for identification purposes. An ID card, commonly referred to as the national ID card, is issued by banks and post offices. The possession of this card is not required; however, its use is widespread. The other card is the drivers license issued by the county board. The issue, manufacture and use of these documents is carefully controlled by the Swedish government. Both require inputs from the Civic Registration Office at the parish of domicile. Drivers licenses require doctors and police board certificates. These documents are issued by the "AB-ID-Kort," a quasi-governmental company. Company ID cards produced for internal use are also accepted for check transactions.

Sweden claims to have minimal problems with fraud (including that related to false identity). The Swedish police in 1975 recorded a total of 23,807 cases of fraud of which 1,198 involved the use of identity cards.[4] In comparison to other countries supplying similar statistics, this incidence rate of approximately 15 per 100,000 persons is considerate moderate. Sweden has moderately strong laws (up to two years imprisonment) governing most manners of misuse of identity documents.

United Kingdom

The United Kingdom has no form of population register, family register or any other systematic method of maintaining a controlled information file on personal identities. There is no national identity document. The document that most closely approximates a national ID is the national insurance health card, which is issued to all employed persons (citizen or alien) and has an assigned card number which is maintained for life. Drivers licenses or other similar commonly used documents have some credibility for establishing identity. In reviewing passport applications, the British rely more on investigative techniques and on countersignatures by private or government officials of some stature (Ministers, Bank Officers, Police Officers, etc.) attesting to applicants' identity than on documents.

The United Kingdom has an exceptionally severe problem of false identity due to the presence of many non-citizens. By longstanding tradition, citizens of British Commonwealth countries have the privileges of relatively free access. Residents of the European Economic Community are also permitted relatively easy entrance. The United Kingdom has different identification rules for each category of aliens. Commonwealth citizens need only national passports; citizens of Common Market countries use national passports, national identity documents or residents permits. Other aliens are required to obtain police registration certificates.

British laws pertinent to false identity vary in severity. Forgery of birth certificates with intent to defraud or deceive can be punished with up to fourteen years imprisonment, whereas forgery of a license is punishable by a maximum of four months imprisonment or 100 pounds fine. The more severe penalties are seldom imposed.

Although the United Kingdom Passport Office states that there is no widespread practice of misuse of United Kingdom documents of identity, Scotland Yard (through INTERPOL) describes numerous documents (birth certificates, social security cards, passports, credit cards, etc.) which are frequently used as a means of establishing a false identity.

West Germany

West Germany occupies a position midway between countries like Sweden which have highly integrated, sophisticated personal identification systems and those like the United Kingdom or the United States in which there is no organized system for personal identification.

West Germany is a federation of more or less independent states; however, certain functions, which in the United States are in the exclusive jurisdiction of the states, are subject in West Germany to a considerable degree of centralized control. West Germany has a national identity document; however, it is not required to be carried at all times and other identity cards (student ID cards, drivers licenses) are satisfactory for many routine identifications within the country. All legal personal records are kept at the place of birth in the office of personal records, an office of the local police. Passports, identity cards and birth certificates are issued by that office, and death certificates are forwarded to that office from anywhere in Germany (East or West) and most other countries in Europe. Although drivers licenses are issued by local authorities, there are plans to produce them using a standardized "forgery proof" synthetic paper to be issued and numbered consecutively by the Federal Printing Establishment. Their issuance will be coordinated with car registration by the "Federal Vehicle Office."

West Germany has a comprehensive set of laws with rather severe penalties covering misuse of identity documents. West Germany maintains no statistics on falsification of identity documents; however, 22,749 cases of forgery of documents were recorded in 1974. In comparison to other countries for which similar statistics are available, this incidence of approximately 36 per 100,000 persons is considered moderate.

Japan

The Japanese system of personal identification has some unique features. Two of these are the use of family registers or "Koseki" and the use of official or private seals or "Jitsuin." The system of "Koseki" is highly developed in Japan and all Japanese nationals are registered at a city, town or village office. The "Koseki" is a unique system of family records which is thirteen centuries old. The Family Registration Law of December 22, 1947 requires the mayor of a city, town or village where the family makes its permanent domicile to keep an accurate record of all changes in the personal status of a specific individual, and any changes in the personal status not entered into the "Koseki" are not recognized as legal in Japan. This "Koseki" is customarily and widely used for identification purposes in Japan.

Government offices in Japan require individualized personal seals on all documents presented to them. Seals are used for cashing checks at banks, postal money orders at post offices, etc. For local purposes a specific seal, called "Jitsuin," which is registered with the mayor of the city, town or village in which the residence of the individual is located, must be presented. This "Jitsuin" is customarily and widely accepted as a means of identification.

Japanese government offices tend to require a combination of three or more items for the purpose of identification; some offices require, as an additional precaution, submission of a postcard which has been mailed to the legal address of the individual concerned and which must be presented at the time the service is requested. This trend is accepted and followed by private concerns such as insurance companies, banks, etc. as well. Items usually required for identification are:

a. "Koseki" (Family Register)
b. "Jitsuin" (Seal)
c. Automobile Drivers License
d. Inhabitants' Certificate
e. Rice Ration Book
f. Health Insurance Certificate
g. Private Identification Cards.

The inhabitants' certificate is issued by the mayor of the city, town or village to each inhabitant in his jurisdiction. The Rice Ration Book is a historically important document no longer extensively used as a basis of identification.

The Japanese believe that the "Koseki" system makes it virtually impossible to mistakenly issue an identification document to an individual who is either dead, missing, or for any other reason, is not the individual he claims to be. The sole exception is a case in which an individual falsely uses someone else's identity with that person actively cooperating.

Japan has a comprehensive set of laws which imposes penalties which should be real deterrents for crimes involving false identity. Of special interest are those crimes involving misuse of seals that are more severely punished than corresponding ones in which seals are not involved. Japan in 1974 recorded 500 cases of obtaining drivers licenses using false identity documents, and 854 cases of illegal use or altering of credit cards. A total of 4,607 cases of falsification of documents were known to police. This incidence of 4.3 cases per 100,000 persons is considered low in comparison to other countries which provided similar statistics.

Brazil

Brazil uses a national identification document and is known to be in the process of establishing a centralized population register system.[4] The national identity document (Cedula) is a wallet-sized, laminated card containing a photograph and thumbprint as well as normal personal identification information and the assigned personal identification number. It is issued to all citizens 18 years of age or older except those possessing identification cards issued to civilian employees and military personnel of the Armed Forces by local identification offices operated by the Department of Public Security in each state. These offices are subject to the policy guidance of the National Institute of Identification, a division of the Federal Police. Aliens are issued permanent or temporary Alien Identity Cards very similar to the Cedula.

Births and deaths are registered by offices of Civil Registry which are established by Federal license on the basis of local need and population. Drivers licenses are issued by local offices of

State Department of Transportation. There is no procedure at present for matching deaths and births. The establishment of the population register system should alleviate this problem somewhat.

Brazil operates under a uniform penal code which provides moderate penalties (with the exceptions of fines which have become ridiculously low due to inflation) for most potential misuses of identity documents. Brazil is in the process of changing these fines to a system in which the judge, within limits set by law, determines the value of fines in terms of multiples of the minimum daily wage in accordance with the financial condition of the guilty party. False identification is considered to be a normal concommitant to other primary types of criminal activity, and there are no statistics available on the extent of this problem.

SECTION V

SUMMARY AND CONCLUSIONS

This report provides a general overview of the problem of false identification in commission of criminal acts in selected foreign countries. It is based primarily on surveys made by the State Department through U.S. embassies abroad and by the International Criminal Police Organization (INTERPOL). Through these surveys and use of other sources of information, it has been possible to provide a reasonably comprehensive description of the false identification problem in twelve of the twenty-five countries on which significant information has been obtained. These twelve countries are mostly Western European or other highly developed countries with which the U.S. has extensive political, social and economic relations. This description is not necessarily representative of a worldwide situation, nor does it cover certain other countries such as Canada and Mexico with which significant common problems of false identity could be anticipated. The extent of the false ID problem in these nations, and the effectiveness of the countermeasures used, is based primarily on the perceptions of the respondents to the survey.

The practices and procedures for personal identification vary greatly from country to country. The countries surveyed tend to fall into one of the following three categories:

1. Countries with strong systems of population registration and personal identification. (Denmark, the Netherlands, Norway, Sweden and Finland).

2. Countries with no highly centralized systems for personal identification characterized by a considerable amount of independence at lower levels of government and little coordination between governmental activities. (Australia and the United Kingdom).

3. Countries which are intermediate between the above two extremes. (Argentina, Brazil, Columbia, France, West Germany, Greece, Japan, Spain).

Those countries which appear to have the least problems with false identification tend to use a combination of techniques designed to counteract each common method of misuse of identity documents. Some form of population registration system and thorough investigative procedures are used to minimize the possibility of a person obtaining an identity document by use of false information or fraudulently obtained supporting documentation. The content of identity documents and techniques used for their fabrication are selected to make forgery or alteration difficult. Penalties against all common methods of misuse of identity documents, sufficiently severe to provide a real deterrent, are established by law.

The greatest emphasis is normally placed on the systematic use of population registration systems. These can vary from highly automated systems with central population registers to manual systems maintained at the local level. The essential ingredients of an effective system are:

a. A single file containing significant information affecting the status of each registered individual.

b. A positive determination of legal residence or domicile for each individual.

c. Consistent use supported by law and practice of the personal file as a required reference for legal actions affecting status.

d. A procedure for regularly updating and verifying the personal file both on an individual and a collective basis.

The prime motivating force behind establishment of population registration systems is administrative efficiency and assurance of equity in establishing tax and voting rolls, etc.; their value as a means of minimizing the problem of false identification is an essential by-product of their establishment.

A unique personal number is normally assigned to each registered individual. This number by itself is a powerful means of identification.

In most countries with population registration systems (and some without) a national identity document of some form is used. In these countries this document is normally the primary means of identification. Where a national identity document does not exist, there is a tendency for some other form of commonly used document (social security, national health insurance cards, etc.) to be used as a partial substitute. Drivers licenses, commercial identity cards, etc. are also used in varying degrees for general identification.

Three countries are known to use family registers, a document maintained by local officials in which all births, deaths, marriages, and other important status information are entered, as a fundamental basis for issuing identity documents.

The most common supporting documents used as a basis for obtaining identity documents are birth and marriage certificates.

Many countries tend to emphasize procedures for investigating and processing applications as a fundamental method for assuring the authenticity of identity documents. Procedures commonly used include requirements for applications to be reviewed at the local level where officials may have personal knowledge of the applicant's identity, careful comparison of statements on applications with data in the applicant's personal/family register, and mailing notifications to receive approved documents to applicant at his legal residence as indicated in his personal record files.

Personal identification practices, to be effective, must be suitable for the country involved. They can become effective only if accepted by the population and integrated into the administrative machinery of the country concerned. Generally, a relatively long time is required to institute and perfect the operation of new procedures.

Some consideration should be given to future expansion of the effort described in this report to create a more authoritative reference document. This effort could take the direction of:

a. Expansion of the coverage to include more countries, particularly all those with which problems involving false identification could be anticipated (i.e., Canada, Mexico, etc.).

b. Developing a detailed, country-by-country descriptive list of all identity documents commonly used together with suggested methods for assuring their validity.

c. In-depth study of population register systems and their relation to the identification process.

d. Determination of specific suggestions for international coordination to minimize the possibility of international crimes involving false identity.

ATTACHMENT A

INTERPOL QUESTIONNAIRE

I. INTRODUCTION

A. Methods used to gather data.

1. List surveys conducted, numbers and types of organizations.

2. List and describe other data sources.

3. List areas in which adequate data could not be obtained and why.

B. List areas which require further investigation or data gathering.

II. DESCRIPTION OF THE FALSE IDENTIFICATION PROBLEM

A. Kinds of transactions of interest to the Task Forces.

1. "Application" phase.

a. List the types of documents applied for and give a general description of the application processes for each.

b. List documents which are applied for and give an estimate of number of applications per year and the number falsely applied for.

Document	No. of applications per year	No. of false applications
________	________	________

c. For each type of document applied for, what types of identity documents is the applicant asked to produce? (If none are required, why are they not required?) Which of these are most frequently involved in false applications?

Document applied for ______________________________.

Identity Document	Check if requested of applicant	Check if frequently used in false I.D.
1. Birth certificate	________	________
2. Social security card	________	________
3. Drivers License	________	________
4. Credit cards Retail-Travel Bank-	________	________
5. Employer I.D. card	________	________
6. Selective Service card	________	________
7. Military I.D. card	________	________
8. Military discharge papers	________	________
9. Immigration & Naturalization papers	________	________
10. Passport	________	________
11. References	________	________
12. None	________	________
13. Other-Specify	________	________

d. Is the authenticity of these documents verified with these sources as a part of the application approval process?

2. "Use" Phase

a. Describe, in general, the ways applicants use documents issued to them.

b. List the uses. For each use estimate the total scope of such use and the scope of fraudulent use.

Use (List)	Total scope of use (Dollar volume, number of uses, or both, etc.)	Scope of fraudulent use (Same units)	Percentage of fraudulent use
________	________	________	________
________	________	________	________
________	________	________	________

c. For each document and type of use, indicate what supporting identification documents, if any, are similtaneously requested of user:

Type of document ______________________.

Use ______________________.

Identity Document	Check if requested
1. Birth certificate	________
2. Social Security Card	________
3. Drivers License	________
4. Credit Card Retail-Travel-Bank	________
5. Employer identification card	________
6. Selective Service Card	________
7. Military Identification card	________
8. Military Discharge Papers	________
9. Immigration & Naturalization Papers	________
10. Passport	________
11. References	________
12. None	________
13. Other - Specify	________

d. In all of the fraudulent uses of each type of document what fraction can be classified as:

   1. Altered ________

   2. Counterfeit ________

   3. Imposter ________

e. Describe which false identification techniques are most common and least common, and which are the most and least successful and why?

B. Give profiles of users of false identity documents.

   1. Age

   2. sex

   3. race

   4. education level

   5. prior criminal record (including types of crimes)

   6. employed or unemployed

   7. residence (rural, suburban, urban)

C. Give other false identity "use" data.

   1. Principal geographical areas

   2. Season of year

   3. State of national or regional economy

   4. Other patterns of use.

D. Give profiles of victims of criminal use of false identification as in B above. Which victims is it used most and least successfully against and why?

E. What is the social, psychological, political or other cost of the obtaining and use of false identification?

F. What is the impact of the use of no identification where it might be used as a tool to deter crime?

G. How many false identification investigations, prosecutions, and declinations were there? Include data for prosecutions.

H. Total estimated administrative costs, including, but not limited to salaries, benefits, transportation, overhead, etc., for the purpose of investigation, prosecution and recovery activities break out costs for cases for the years 1970-1974 if data is available.

I. Please attach copies of the forms used for the referral of the fraud cases and reporting of fraud investigative activities.

III. COUNTERMEASURES TO CRIMINAL USE OF FALSE IDENTIFICATION

A. For each document which you issue, list the countermeasures which are presently employed or about to be employed, together with specific estimates of cost and effectiveness of each countermeasure.

1. For the "application" phase.

2. For the "use" phase.

B. <u>Preliminary Recommendations</u> - List your preliminary recommendations for combating the obtaining and use of false identification.

For each document which you issue, list additional countermeasure which could be taken and evaluate each as cost, effectiveness, and other relevant criteria such as acceptability to the public.

IV. OTHER COMMENTS

V. ATTACHMENTS

Please attach all relevant supporting data, including:

a. Synopses of selected criminal false identification cases.
b. Copies of statutes, if any, that set forth penalties for individuals who provide others with false identification documents. What efforts are made to enforce the provisions of such statutes?
c. Copies of statutes, if any, that prevent or limit verification and reporting of false identification to law enforcement officials (e.g., confidentiality statutes prohibiting disclosure of information by employees to law enforcement officials).

ATTACHMENT B

STATE DEPARTMENT QUESTIONNAIRE

1. Is there a standard identification document in use in your country?

2. If the answer to #1 is affirmative, describe briefly the procedure used to issue the document including the method of establishing identity, the type of documents issued, and the agency responsible for the task.

   NOTE: If possible, furnish copies of laws and regulations, application forms, and the document or documents issued.

3. If the answer to question #1 is negative, state how a person's identity is generally established in your country.

4. Does the identification system differ with regard to citizens, resident aliens and temporary aliens? If so, describe the system used for each category.

5. What is the primary issuing agency for:

   a. Birth Certificates
   b. Death Certificates
   c. Drivers' Licenses

6. Is there any system at this time for matching death certificates with birth certificates? If so, please describe in detail, and estimate its effectiveness in preventing fraudulent use of birth certificates.

7. What are the present legal penalties for fraudulent obtention or use of birth certificates, drivers' licenses, and other identity documents.

8. What is the present legislative trend or attitude regarding penalties for fraudulent use of personal identity documents?

9. Is there any mutual cooperation between this nation and other nations regarding enforcement of legal penalties, and investigation of fraudulent obtention or use of identity documents?

10. Is there any legislation presently in force similar to our Privacy Act which would protect the privacy of personal information given to obtain personal identity documents? If so, please describe.

11. While statistics would be extremely useful to our Committee, it is realized that these may be impossible to obtain. It would be helpful however, if you could relate the circumstances of any widespread practice or any important cases which had wide publicity.

COMMENT: If it would be helpful in obtaining this information, you may inform the local government that the Committee will be pleased to furnish it with its final report which will include the scope of the problem as well as recommended solutions.

Please translate any information which is given other than pamphlets, laws and regulations.

ATTACHMENT C

EXTRACT FROM FRENCH CRIMINAL CODE

Article 153 (Ord. nr 58-1298 of 23 Dec. 1958). "Whosoever counterfeits, falsifies or alters permits, certificates memorandum books, cards, official reports, receipts, passports, laisser-passer or other documents issued by public administrations in order to verify an identity or a position, or to grant an authorization, will be punished by imprisonment of from six months to one year and fined from 1500 to 15000 francs."

The guilty party will also be denied the rights mentioned in Article 42 of this Code for at least five years and with a maximum of ten years counting from the day of his conviction.

The attempt will be punished in the same way as the completed action.

The same punishment will be applicable to:

1. He who made use of counterfeit, falsified or altered documents.

2. He who uses one of the documents described in the first paragraph when the data provided by the subject have become incomplete or incorrect.

Article 154 (Ord. nr 58-1298 of 23 Dec. 1958) "Whosoever unduly has issued to himself, or attempts to have issued any of the documents described in the preceding article, either by making false statements, by taking a false name or position, or by furnishing false information, certificates or affidavits will be punished by imprisonment of from three months to two years and fined from 500 to 5000 francs."

The same sentences will be applied to he who has used such a document, either obtained through the aforementioned conditions or made out in a name other than his own.

The official who issues or causes to have issued one of the documents covered by the preceding article to a person that he knows does not have rights to it, will be punished by imprisonment of from one to four years and fined from 1500 to 15000 francs, without prejudice to more severe sentence he might be given through application of articles 177 and those following. The guilty party might also be denied the rights mentioned in article 42 of this Code for at least five years and with a maximum of ten years from the date of his conviction.

LIST OF REFERENCES

1. Record file of replies from U.S. embassies in twelve countries to the Department of State's Operations Memoranda of January 22 and March 26, 1976, subject: "Information for Federal Advisory Commission," maintained by the office of William E. Duggan, Deputy Director for Legal and Security Affairs Passport Office (PTT/U). Duplicate working file at The MITRE Corporation, Bedford, Massachusetts.

2. Record file of replies from INTERPOL offices in sixteen foreign countries to letter dated, 15 July 1975, Number 100, Survey 55, maintained in the office of Louis B. Sims, Chief, International Criminal Police Organization, USA, National Central Bureau, Department of the Treasury. Duplicate working file at The MITRE Corporation, Bedford, Massachusetts.

3. "International Symposium on Automation of Population Register Systems," Information Processing Association of Israel, Volume I, "Proceedings," Jerusalem, Israel, 25-28 September 1967.

4. 1971 Fall Joint Computer Conference, November 16-18, 1971, American Federation of Information Processing Societies, Conference Proceedings, Volume 39.

Appendix II

Documentary Requirements for Aliens in the United States

The Immigration Service Asks Your Help

In the regular course of daily duties you, as a law enforcement officer or an employer, often come in contact with aliens. All aliens (non-citizens) are subject to immigration laws which regulate their entry and set conditions on their stay. Local law enforcement officers and employers are in a position to help in the enforcement of these laws.

The vast majority of aliens in the United States are legally here. The information herein will help you to identify the various immigration documents that might be carried by an alien who is legally in the U.S. Most aliens lawfully in the United States should have some kind of immigration document. Exceptions: Canadians and certain other residents of Canada may be admitted to the U.S. for periods of up to six months for pleasure or business without the issuance of immigration documents; however, they usually will have in their possession evidence of Canadian citizenship or residence. Other aliens, such as government officials from Mexico or Canada, and employees of treaty organizations such as NATO, are often admitted without documents. They will have some form of official identification, however.

Some aliens have entered this country illegally, and in addition, others who were given permission to enter temporarily have violated the conditions of their admission. These aliens are "wanted" by the Immigration and Naturalization Service. It is not the purpose of this chapter to authorize the arrest or detention of any person, but if an alien comes to your attention who *appears* to be in illegal status, or you wish further information, you are requested to telephone or wire "collect" to the nearest office of the Immigration and Naturalization Service. Your call will be appreciated and will be given prompt attention.

Generally speaking, all persons in the United States are either citizens or aliens.

Citizens

All persons born in the United States are, with rare exceptions, United States citizens. U.S. citizenship can also be acquired by naturalization through court proceedings or by certain persons born abroad of U.S. citizen parents. Long residence in this country or marriage to a citizen do not by themselves confer citizenship on an alien.

There are some ways a person can lose citizenship, such as naturalization in a foreign country, formal renunciation, etc., if those acts were voluntarily performed with an intent to relinquish United States citizenship.

United States citizens are not required to carry evidence of citizenship such as birth or naturalization certificates. However, most persons have some means of identification, particularly those who speak English with difficulty.

Aliens

Generally, any person not a citizen of the United States is an alien. All aliens may be grouped as follows (this summary of a portion of the immigration laws is not intended for use as a legal reference):

1. *Immigrants*—aliens who have been admitted for permanent residence. They can remain indefinitely, own property, work, and move about without restriction as they comply with the laws relating to alien registration, changes of address and annual reports. Such aliens may become subject to deportation, however, if they (1) are convicted of certain crimes, (2) engage in subversive or immoral activity, or (3) become public charges. All are required to have Alien Registration Receipt Cards.

An alien coming to the United States for permanent residence is issued an immigrant visa by the Department of State at an office outside the U.S. It is a separate document which is surrendered to the Immigration and Naturalization Service at the port of entry and made a part of the Service's record relating to the alien as evidence of his lawful admission for permanent residence.

2. *Nonimmigrants*—aliens admitted temporarily for specific purposes and periods of time. They are generally required to carry a Form I-94 endorsed to show their status. The I-94 will bear one of the following letters indicating the status and will have a number after it (i.e. B-2, H-3, J-1, etc.):

A. Foreign government officials on official business and their families and servants.

B. Visitors for business or pleasure. "Business" does not include accepting employment in the United States.

C. Aliens in travel status while traveling directly through the United States.

D. Alien crewmen who may be given shore leave while their ship is in port, or given permission to seek a berth on another vessel. In no event may the time limit exceed 29 days.

E. Treaty traders and investors and their families.

F. Alien students admitted to attend specified schools. Students may accept employment only with written permission.

G. Representatives and personnel of international organizations and their families and servants.

H. Temporary workers, including agricultural laborers.

I. Members of foreign press, radio, film, or other information media and their families.

J. Exchange visitors who are here under Department of State approved programs of study, teaching research or training.

K. Fiances and Fiancees of United States citizens and their children.

L. Intra-company transferees and their families.

Except for those aliens admitted specifically to work, such as agricultural laborers, nonimmigrant aliens normally may not accept employment within the United States. Students and exchange visitors may, with written permission, accept certain employment.

A nonimmigrant alien is subject to deportation and "wanted" by the Immigration and Naturalization Service if the alien violates the terms of admission: abandons status, overstays the period of admission, engages in criminal, immoral, narcotic or subversive activity, or accepts unauthorized employment.

3. *Parolees*—aliens not otherwise admissible who are sometimes paroled into the United States at the discretion of the government. They are required to carry a Form I-94 endorsed to show their parole status. Employment is permitted in most instances.

4. *Illegal entrants*—those aliens who were not admitted to the U.S. for either temporary or permanent stay, but entered in such a manner or place as to avoid inspection. These aliens are deportable. All illegal entrants are "wanted" by the Immigration and Naturalization Service.

An alien in an illegal status may present a false or altered card or document or, more frequently, an authentic one belonging to someone else. The first step is to determine if the holder is actually the person named on the document. Next, each document issued by the Immigration and Naturalization Service will show the conditions of admission. Often, from examining these documents and briefly questioning the alien, it can be determined that he/she does not appear to be in legal status. The most common violations of temporary admissions are working when employment has not been authorized, and remaining beyond the time to which admitted.

Aliens who have entered surreptitiously and have not been apprehended by the Immigration and Naturalization Service will not rightfully be in possession of valid documents. However, they often claim legal status or even United States citizenship and fraudulently present some sort of documentation to substantiate their claims.

Nonimmigrant Visa

There are several types of nonimmigrant visas. Two of these types are seen below.

Frequently the expression "when my visa expires" is erroneously used to mean "when my period of admission expires." The following may clarify the common misunderstanding.

Temporary (nonimmigrant) visas are issued by the Department of State at offices in foreign countries. Such visa is a stamp placed on one of the pages of the passport, which usually is issued by the country of the alien's nationality. The visa may be of limited or indefinite validity. Possession of the visa does not establish a right to be in or remain in the United States. It is merely a permit to proceed to a United States port of

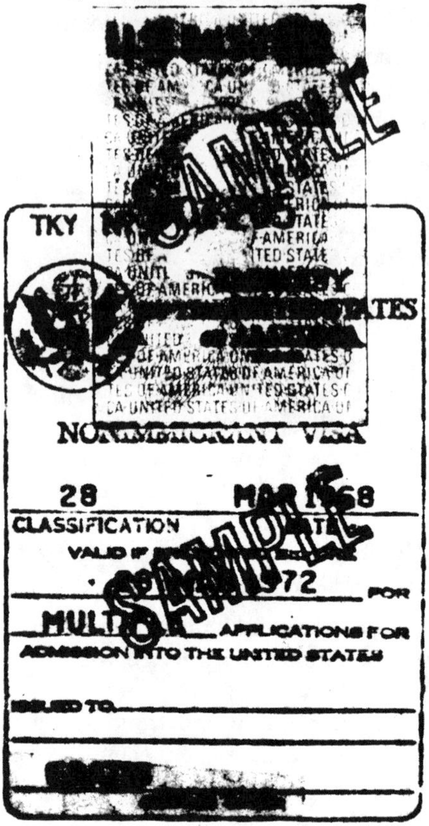

entry to apply to the U.S. Immigration and Naturalization Service for admission into the United States. The conditions and period of admission are decided by the immigration officer at the port of entry after the alien has been interviewed. A Form I-94, Arrival-Departure Record, showing the period of authorized admission, is issued by the immigration officer and stapled in the passport. Any extensions of stay subsequently granted are shown on the reverse of the form, which is surrendered at the time the alien departs the United States.

To be valid the visa must be unexpired when the alien applies at the port of entry. However, the remaining period of the visa's validity has no bearing on the period of authorized admission granted by the immigration officer. For example, an alien might be admitted for six months (and perhaps even receive one or more extensions of stay) even though the visa may have been valid for only one day beyond the date on which he/she applied for admission. On the other hand, an alien's admission might be limited to one week, even though at the time of admission his/her visa may have been valid for four years. Moreover, the alien might be refused entry altogether, notwithstanding the possession of a valid unexpired visa.

If the bearer of a nonimmigrant visa has been admitted into the United States for a temporary period, the alien should also have in possession evidence of his admission and of the terms of such admission. This evidence will usually consist of Form I-94. However, some aliens who are here on temporary visits may have a Form I-94 but no visa.

Alien Registration Receipt Cards

Form AR-3a, shown on the next two pages, was issued from 1941 to 1949. It is not absolute evidence of legal permanent residence; however, the holder is porbably not deportable. Employment in the United States is permitted.

Aliens lawfully admitted into the United States for permanent residence should be in possession of either Form I-151 or Form I-551 Alien Registraion Receipt Cards. Form I-151 (shown below) was last revised on 7/1/72 and has a background printing of many small blue circles. Older issues may have a slightly different format and contained either blue or black printing on a background of blue and yellow overlays, or black printing on a light green background. All have a form number and are laminated in plastic. Employment in the U.S. is permitted.

Form I-551 (shown below) has replaced Form I-151, but both types are valid evidence that an alien has been admitted for permanent residence. The Form I-551 contains the lawful holder's photograph, fingerprint and signature with blue printing superimposed over a white background. Employment is permitted.

FORM AR-3a (ALIEN REGISTRATION RECEIPT CARD)

Front—Actual Size

Form AR-3a

Registration Number 6962241

W - 282265

ALIEN REGISTRATION RECEIPT CARD

John J. Doe
1313 Main Ave.
Atlanta, Ga.

SAMPLE

KEEP THIS CARD. Keep a record of the number.

UNITED STATES DEPARTMENT OF JUSTICE
IMMIGRATION AND NATURALIZATION SERVICE
ALIEN REGISTRATION DIVISION
WASHINGTON, D. C.

To the Registrant:

Your registration under the Alien Registration Act, 1940, has been received and given the number shown above your name. This card is your receipt, and is evidence only of such registration. In writing to the Department of Justice about yourself, always give the number on this card.

GPO 16—1641 Director of Registration.

FORM AR-3a (ALIEN REGISTRATION RECEIPT CARD)

Reverse

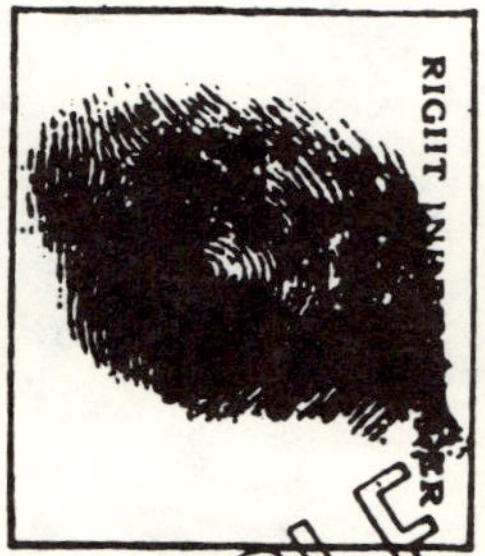

This Alien Registration Receipt Card should be sent to the Alien Registration Division, Department of Justice, Washington, D. C., (1) if it is found; or (2) if the person named hereon departs from the United States, or becomes naturalized, or dies.

SAMPLE

John J Doe

(SIGNATURE OF REGISTRANT, OR PERSON REGISTERING THE ALIEN)

ADDRESS REPORTS—Read Carefully

The Alien Registration Act, 1940, requires all resident aliens to report each change of address within 5 days of such change. Other aliens, for example: Visitors, students, and others not admitted for permanent residence in the United States, must report their address every 3 months whether they change their address or not. Prepared forms for such address changes and reports may be obtained at any post office. A penalty of fine and imprisonment is provided by law for failure to make the required reports. Address letters and reports to the Alien Registration Division, Department of Justice, Washington, D. C.

When reporting, give both your number and name.

U. S. GOVERNMENT PRINTING OFFICE 16—16416

FORM I-151 (ALIEN REGISTRATION RECEIPT CARD)

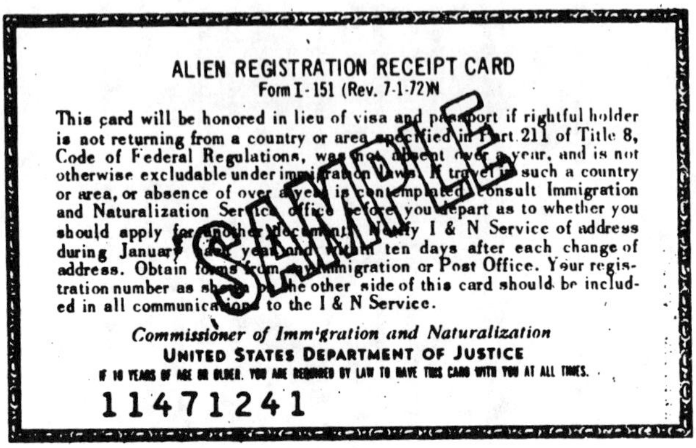
ALIEN REGISTRATION RECEIPT CARD

Form I-151 (Rev. 7-1-72)N

This card will be honored in lieu of visa and passport if rightful holder is not returning from a country or area specified in Part 211 of Title 8, Code of Federal Regulations, was not absent over a year, and is not otherwise excludable under immigration laws. If travel to such a country or area, or absence of over a year is contemplated consult Immigration and Naturalization Service office before you depart as to whether you should apply for another document. Notify I & N Service of address during January each year and within ten days after each change of address. Obtain forms from any Immigration or Post Office. Your registration number as shown on the other side of this card should be included in all communications to the I & N Service.

Commissioner of Immigration and Naturalization

UNITED STATES DEPARTMENT OF JUSTICE

IF 18 YEARS OF AGE OR OLDER, YOU ARE REQUIRED BY LAW TO HAVE THIS CARD WITH YOU AT ALL TIMES.

11471241

Front—Actual Size

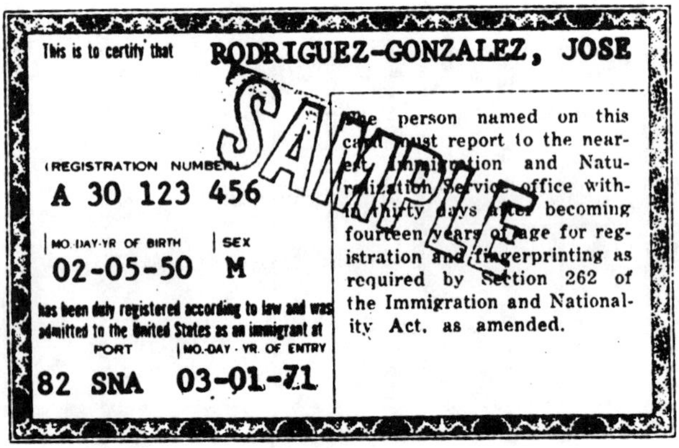
This is to certify that RODRIGUEZ-GONZALEZ, JOSE

(REGISTRATION NUMBER)

A 30 123 456

MO.-DAY-YR. OF BIRTH: 02-05-50

SEX: M

has been duly registered according to law and was admitted to the United States as an immigrant at

PORT: 82 SNA

MO.-DAY-YR. OF ENTRY: 03-01-71

The person named on this card must report to the nearest Immigration and Naturalization Service office within thirty days after becoming fourteen years of age for registration and fingerprinting as required by Section 262 of the Immigration and Nationality Act, as amended.

Reverse

FORM I-551 (ALIEN REGISTRATION RECEIPT CARD)

Front—Actual Size

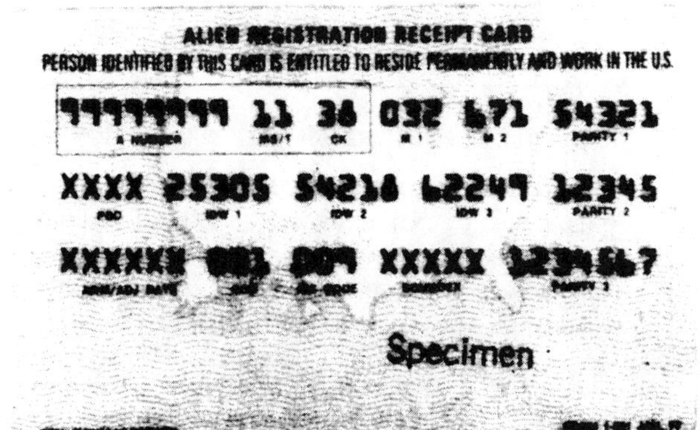

Reverse

Border Crossing Cards

Form I-185 is a Nonresident Alien Canadian Border Crossing Card (shown below). It is issued to Canadian citizens or British subjects residing in Canada to facilitate entry into the U.S. for visiting as nonimmigrant border crossers. The form is printed on pink paper and laminated in plastic. Most Canadian visitors, however, are admitted without documents. Employment in U.S. is *not* permitted.

FORM I-185 (NONRESIDENT ALIEN CANADIAN BORDER CROSSING CARD)

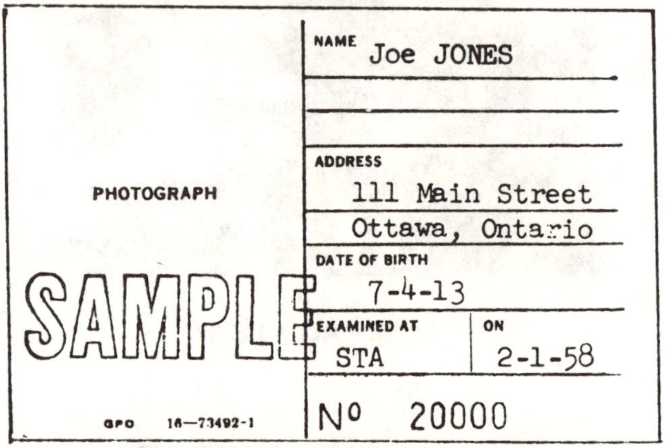
PHOTOGRAPH

SAMPLE

GPO 16—73492-1

NAME Joe JONES

ADDRESS 111 Main Street
Ottawa, Ontario

DATE OF BIRTH 7-4-13

EXAMINED AT STA

ON 2-1-58

Nº 20000

Front—Actual Size

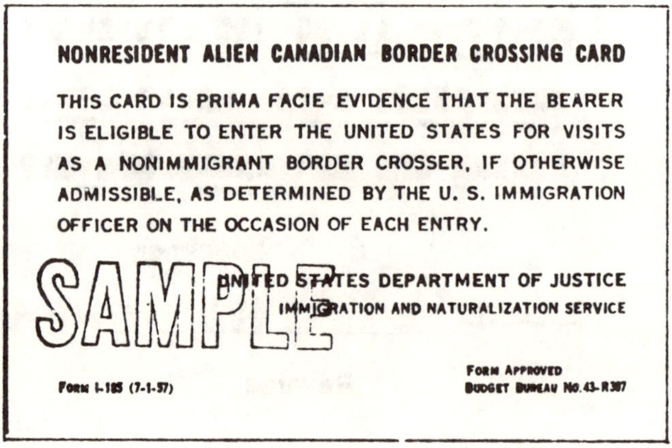
NONRESIDENT ALIEN CANADIAN BORDER CROSSING CARD

THIS CARD IS PRIMA FACIE EVIDENCE THAT THE BEARER IS ELIGIBLE TO ENTER THE UNITED STATES FOR VISITS AS A NONIMMIGRANT BORDER CROSSER, IF OTHERWISE ADMISSIBLE, AS DETERMINED BY THE U. S. IMMIGRATION OFFICER ON THE OCCASION OF EACH ENTRY.

SAMPLE

UNITED STATES DEPARTMENT OF JUSTICE
IMMIGRATION AND NATURALIZATION SERVICE

FORM I-185 (7-1-57)

FORM APPROVED
BUDGET BUREAU NO. 43-R387

Reverse

The Nonresident Alien Canadian Border Crossing Identification Card shown below is issued to nonimmigrant aliens who have been admitted to Canada for permanent residence as "landed immigrants" and seek to enter the U.S. only as temporary visitors for business or pleasure. The "card" is actually a stamp placed in the alien's passport or travel document. The holder may be admitted without requiring a nonimmigrant visa or Form I-94. Employment in the U.S. is *not* permitted.

NONRESIDENT ALIEN CANADIAN BORDER CROSSING IDENTIFICATION CARD

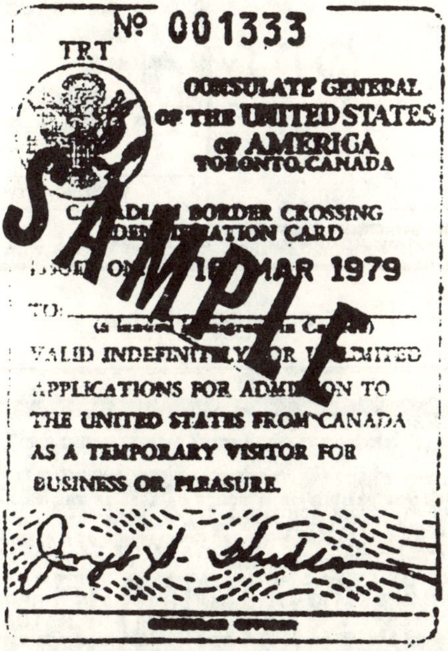

Form I-186, Nonresident Alien Mexican Border Crossing Card, is shown below. It is issued to Mexican citizens for entry into the U.S. as a nonimmigrant for visits not to exceed 72 hours or 25 miles from the Mexican border. For any admission in excess of the above, the alien will have a Form I-444, or in some cases a Form I-94, showing the area and time limitations for admission. The Form I-186 is laminated in plastic. Those issued prior to 9/15/65 were blue and those issued after that date are salmon-beige. Employment in the U.S. is *not* permitted.

FORM I-186 (NONRESIDENT ALIEN MEXICAN BORDER CROSSING CARD)

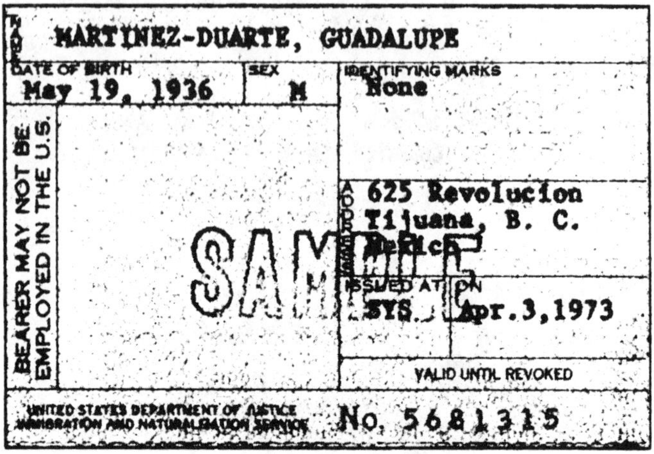

Front—Actual Size

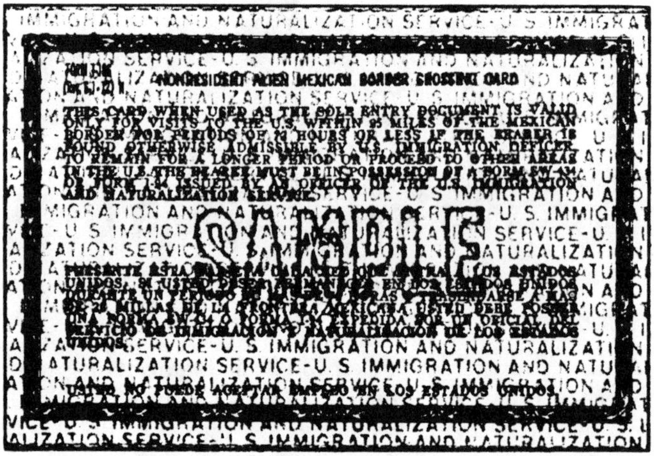

Reverse

Shown below is Form I-444—a Mexican Border Visitor's Permit. It is issued to the rightful holder of a valid form I-186 who has been admitted for a visit for business or pleasure within 25 miles of the Mexican border for a period of more than 72 hours but not more than 15 days or for a visit outside the immediate border area but within the States of Texas, New Mexico, Arizona or California for a period of not more than 15 days. The period of validity is indicated on the admission stamp. The form is printed on safety paper. Employment in the U.S. is *not* permitted.

FORM I–144 (MEXICAN BORDER VISITORS PERMIT)

PERMISO PARA VISITANTES MEXICANOS A ESTADOS FRONTERIZOS DE LOS ESTADOS UNIDOS.

BIENVENIDO A LOS ESTADOS UNIDOS

Queda Ud. autorizado a permanecer en los Estados Unidos en calidad de visitante, sea con motivo de negocios o de recreo, hasta la fecha indicada abajo. Durante este periodo puede Ud. trasladarse a cualquier lugar de los estados de Texas, Nuevo México, Arizona o California. No se le autoriza a aceptar empleo en los Estados Unidos. Retenga este documento junto con su Tarjeta I-186 (mica) hasta que salga de los Estados Unidos.

Si Ud. desea visitar [illegible] fuera de Texas, Nuevo México, Arizona o [illegible] permanecer en los Estados Unidos después de la fecha indicada abajo, consulte con la oficina [illegible] cercana del Servicio de Inmigración y Naturalización de los Estados Unidos.

Form I-186 No. ____

United States Department of Justice

Immigration and Naturalization Service

1329005

Form I-444 (9-1-76)

U.S. IMMIGRATION
939 SYS PE6
1 AUG 1978
ADMITTED B-2
UNTIL AUG 14, 1978

GPO 279-823

FORM I-94 (ARRIVAL-DEPARTURE RECORD)

Family Name *(Capital Letters)*: SANTOS | First Name: MARIA | Middle Initial: G. | S-550

Country of Citizenship: El Salvador | Passport or Alien Registration Number: G 980356

• United States Address *(Number, Street, City and State)*: 4900 Del Plaza Street, Fairfax, Virginia 22045

• • Airline and Flight No. or Vessel of Arrival: PANAM [illegible] | • • Passenger Boarded at: SAN SALVADOR

Number, Street, City, Province (State) and Country of Permanent Residence: 35 Marion Street, San Salvador, El Salvador

Month, Day and Year of Birth: May 13, 1948

City, Province *(State)* and Country of Birth: San Salvador, El Salvador

Visa Issued at: San Salvador, El Salvador

STAPLE HERE | Month, Day and Year Visa Issued: March 11, 1979

U.S. IMMIGRATION 250

SEP 0 4 1979

ADMITTED B-2 (CLASS)

UNTIL Nov. 4, 1979

ACCEPTS UNAUTHORIZED EMPLOYMENT IS SUBJECT TO DEPORTATION

When Leaving The United States SEE REVERSE

FOR I-94

Front—Actual Size

IMPORTANT NOTICE

- Retain this permit in your possession.
- The validity date of your visa does not mean you have permission to remain in the U.S. for such time.
- You are authorized to stay in the U.S. only until the date inscribed by the inspector on this form. To remain past this date, without permission from Immigration authorities, is a violation of law.

WHEN YOU LEAVE THE UNITED STATES

- By sea or air, surrender this permit to transportation line.
- Over Canadian border, surrender this permit to Canadian Immigration Officer.
- Over Mexican border, surrender this permit to United States Immigration Officer.

RECORD OF EXTENSIONS

To ____ Office ____

To ____ Office ____

To ____ Office ____

DEPARTURE RECORD

Port:

Date:

Carrier:

To:

(Country of disembarkation)

UNITED STATES DEPARTMENT OF JUSTICE
Immigration and Naturalization Service

Reverse

Form I-94: Arrival-Departure Record

The above Form I-94 is issued to aliens admitted temporarily and shows the date to which admitted and any extensions thereof. Generally, employment in the U.S. is not permitted unless the Immigration and Naturalization Service has endorsed the form to so indicate.

FORM 1-94 (ARRIVAL-DEPARTURE RECORD) (PAROLE EDITION)

amily Name *(Capital Letters)* DUMAS | First Name Keith | Middle Initial A | D-520

ountry of Citizenship Jamaica | Passport or Alien Registration Number #15772

nited States Address *(Number, Street, City and State)* 727 West 11th Street, Indianapolis, Indiana

irline and Flight No. or Vessel of Arrival BWIA #402 | Passenger Boarded at Kingston Jamaica

umber, Street, City, Province (State) and Country of Permanent Residence 16 Randwick Drive, Kingston, Jamaica (all 150 607)

onth, Day and Year of Birth September 13, 1932 | PAROLED PURSUANT TO SEC. 212 (d)(5) OF THE I & N ACT TO: November 20, 1980

ity, Province *(State)* and Country of Birth St, Ann, Jamaica | PURPOSE: 1st preference beneficiary

isa Issued at (I-512)

STAPLE HERE | Month, Day and Year Visa Issued | (Port) HMM | (Date) 12/22/79 | (Officer) JGH

SURRENDER THIS COPY WHEN LEAVING THE UNITED STATES—SEE REVERSE

FORM I-94

SAMPLE

Front—Actual Size

Your parole into the United States does not constitute an admission under the terms of the Immigration and Nationality Act. You must observe the conditions of the parole and failure to comply with any of those conditions may result in the revocation of your parole. If, for any reason, you do not proceed to the address shown on the face of this form, or if after arrival, you change your address you must immediately report to the nearest office of the Immigration and Naturalization Service. You must also report to the nearest office of the Immigration and Naturalization Service if your status is not otherwise changed or if you do not leave the United States before the termination date shown.

UPON DEPARTURE FROM THE UNITED STATES

- By sea or air surrender this permit to transportation line.
- Over Canadian border, surrender this permit to Canadian Immigration Officer.
- Over Mexican border, surrender this permit to United States Immigration Officer.

DEPARTURE RECORD

Port:

Date:

Carrier:

To:
(Country of disembarkation)

UNITED STATES DEPARTMENT OF JUSTICE
Immigration and Naturalization Service
Form Approved Budget Bureau No. 43-R311.7
ARRIVAL — DEPARTURE RECORD
FORM I-94 (Rev. 6-1-79)Y (Parole Edition)

Reverse

The Form I-94 shown above is issued to aliens who have been paroled into the U.S. and shows the date to which paroled and other limitations. Employment is not permitted unless the Immigration and Naturalization Service has endorsed the form to so indicate.

FORM I-95A (CREWMAN'S LANDING PERMIT)
Front—Actual Size

Family name	Given name	Initial	Soundex
Turner	James	N.	T-656

Home address and name of relative or friend residing there #10 Downing Street London, England - William Turner (Father)

Address in the U.S. Smith & Jones Agents, Baltimore, Maryland

Date and place of birth: January 1, 1922 London, England

Hair	Eyes	Height	Weight	Sex
BLK.	BRN.	5'10"	170	☒ M ☐ F

A. No. A15335322

Action by Immigration Officer

Washington, D. C. D-1

You are required to depart from U. S. on next sailing of named vessel. You may not be paid off or discharged in the U. S. In no event is stay authorized beyond 29 days.

Passport (No. and Nationality) 4236 British

Arrived by S/S North Star

MAY 12 1966 WAS 3

U. S. Immigration Officer

Form Approved
Budget Bureau No. 43R 360.3

Form I-95A (Rev. 9-1-64)
CREWMAN'S LANDING PERMIT

ANY HANDWRITTEN ENTRIES MUST BE IN BLOCK CAPITAL LETTERS

SAMPLE

U. S. DEPARTMENT OF JUSTICE
IMMIGRATION AND NATURALIZATION SERVICE

By accepting this conditional permit to land the holder agrees to all the conditions incident to the issuance thereof, and to deportation from the United States in accordance with the provisions of section 252(b) of the Immigration and Nationality Act.

DATE OF ARRIVAL	PLACE OF ARRIVAL	SIGNATURE OF IMMIGRATION OFFICER
JUN 20 1966		WAS 3

SAMPLE

Reverse

The Form I-94 shown above is issued to alien crewmen admitted for a period not to exceed 29 days from last arrival either as a "D-1" which requires departure on the same vessel, or "D-2" which permits reshipping on another vessel. Employment in the U.S. is *not* permitted.

Recommended Reading

Anyone interested in fake I.D. can learn a lot from reading the following publications:

CRIMINAL USE OF FALSE IDENTIFICATION. Loompanics Unlimited, PO Box 1197, Port Townsend, WA 98368. *A reprint of the U.S. Government report on false identification.*

DIRECTORY OF MAIL DROPS IN THE UNITED STATES AND CANADA, With An Appendix For Foreign Countries, ***compiled by Michael Hoy.*** Loompanics Unlimited, P.O. Box 1197, Pt. Townsend, WA 98368. *Just what the title says. More than 700 mail drops all over the world are listed, with complete information on the services offered by each.*

DRIVERS LICENSE GUIDE. Drivers License Guide Company, 1492 Oddstad Drive, Redwood City, CA 94063. *This book contains actual-size, full-color photographs of all currently valid Canadian driver's licenses, with explanations of coding systems.*

HOW DRIVER'S LICENSES ARE MADE WITH THE POLAROID CAMERA, ***by Carl Dorski.*** Roadrunner Publications, PO Box 2375, Ft. Pierce, FL 33454. *This book reveals an ingenious cheap method for counterfeiting nearly any kind of I.D. card.*

HOW TO FIND MISSING PERSONS, ***by Ronald George Eriksen 2.*** Loompanics Unlimited, PO Box 1197, Port Townsend, WA 98368. *This book is the best ever written on tracking down missing persons. These are the tricks and methods investigators will use to find you.*

HOW TO LAUNDER MONEY, ***by John Gregg.*** Loompanics Unlimited, PO Box 1197, Pt. Townsend, WA 98368. *This book contains a detailed chapter on taking over the identity of a living person.*

I.D. FOR SALE, ***compiled by Michael Hoy.*** Loompanics Unlimited, PO Box 1197, Pt. Townsend, WA 98368. *A complete guide to the mail order I.D. industry, with many photos, and even a section on I.D.-making machines.*

METHODS OF DISGUISE, ***by John Sample.*** Loompanics Unlimited, PO Box 1197, Port Townsend, WA 98368. *An excellent illustrated book covering all methods of disguise, from simple makeup to plastic surgery.*

NEW I.D. IN AMERICA, ***by Anonymous.*** Paladin Press, PO Box 1307, Boulder CO 80306. *A good supplement to THE PAPER TRIP I & II (below).*

THE PAPER TRIP I & II, ***by Barry Reid.*** Eden Press, PO Box 8410, Fountain Valley, CA 92708. *Although they only cover getting I.D. in the United States, these are the best books ever written on fake I.D.*

SOCIAL SECURITY PROGRAMS THROUGHOUT THE WORLD. *U.S. Department of Health and Human Services Report No. 58. A useful summary of social security programs around the world.*

TAP NEWSLETTER #50. Tap, Room 603, 147 W. 42nd St., New York, NY 10036. *A newsletter of underground technology, this issue contains an article on how to make counterfeit birth certificates.*

WHEN YOUR MONEY FAILS, 666 and THE NEW MONEY SYSTEM, ***by Mary Relfe.*** Ministries Inc., Montgomery, Alabama. *These are religious books and are heavily oriented towards "the mark of the beast." Even so, they are the best source of information on the new identification systems, such as injectable I.D. and hand-scan machines.*

CONTROVERSIAL AND UNUSUAL BOOKS!!!

"Yes, there are books about the skills of apc alypse -- spying, surveillance, fraud, wire-tappi smuggling, self-defense, lockpicking, gunmansh eavesdropping, car chasing, civil warfare, survivi jail, and dropping out of sight. Apparently writi books is the way mercenaries bring in spare ca between wars. The books are useful, and it's go the information is freely available (and they d initely inspire interesting dreams), but their adv should be taken with a salt shaker or two and your wits. A few of these volumes are truly sca Loompanics is the best of the Libertarian suppli who carry them. Though full of 'you'll-wish-you read-these-when-it's-too-late' rhetoric, their c alog is genuinely informative."

-THE NEXT WHOLE EARTH CATALOG

Now available:
THE BEST BOOK CATALOG IN THE WORLD!!!

- ***Large 8½ x 11 size!***
- ***More than 500 of the most controversial and unusual books ever printed!!!***
- ***YOU can order EVERY book listed!!!***
- ***Periodic Supplements to keep you posted on the LATEST titles available!!!***

We offer hard-to-find books on the world's most unusua subjects. Here are a few of the topics covered IN DEPTH ir our exciting new catalog:

- ***Hiding/concealment of physical objects! A complete section of the best books ever written on hiding things!***
- ***Fake ID/Alternate Identities! The most comprehensive selection o books on this little-known subject ever offered for sale! You have tc see it to believe it!***
- ***Investigative/Undercover methods and techniques! Professiona secrets known only to a few, now revealed for YOU to use! Actua police manuals on shadowing and surveillance!***
- ***And much, much more, including Locks and Locksmithing, Sel Defense, Intelligence Increase, Life Extension, Money-Making Op portunities, and much, much more!***

Our book catalog is truly THE BEST BOOK CATALOG IN THE WORLD! Order yours today -- you will be very pleased we know.

(Our catalog is free with the order of any book on the previous page - or is $2.00 if ordered by itself.)

Loompanics Unlimited
PO Box 1197
Pt Townsend, WA 98368
USA